822.3   88058
Ew5b

DATE DUE			

BURTONIAN MELANCHOLY

IN THE PLAYS OF JOHN FORD

PRINCETON STUDIES IN ENGLISH
EDITED BY G. H. GEROULD
· 19 ·

BURTONIAN MELANCHOLY

IN THE PLAYS OF
JOHN FORD

BY

S. BLAINE EWING

1969
OCTAGON BOOKS
New York

Reprinted 1969
by special arrangement with Princeton University Press

OCTAGON BOOKS
A Division of Farrar, Straus & Giroux, Inc.
19 Union Square West
New York, N. Y. 10003

AM

822.3
E w 5 b
88058
april 1974

Library of Congress Catalog Card Number: 77-96156

Printed in U.S.A. by
TAYLOR PUBLISHING COMPANY
DALLAS, TEXAS

To
M. S. E.
and
D. Q. E.

PREFACE

THIS monograph presents a detailed study of the indebtedness of John Ford's plays to Robert Burton's *Anatomy of Melancholy*. It is an expansion of a part of the author's doctoral dissertation, *John Ford's Tragedies and Tragicomedies* (Princeton 1934). The first section presents an analytical summary of the entire *Anatomy*, beginning with the definition of "melancholy" in the specialized sense used by Burton, and continuing with Burton's own headings and arrangement: Parts Affected, Kinds, Causes, Symptoms, Prognostics, Cure, Heroical Love-Melancholy, Jealous Melancholy, and Religious Melancholy. The second section examines in detail Ford's use of this material, character by character and play by play, thus presenting a great wealth of hitherto unnoted source material. The third section discusses in general the significance of Ford's use of melancholy in the plays: the range of his interest, the exactitude of his comprehension of the theme of melancholy and progress in the treatment of it; and estimates the effect of melancholy upon the characters and action, upon the thought and mood, of the plays. At the last a conjectural explanation of Ford's interest in melancholy is offered.

This investigation of the history of some of Ford's ideas shows now for the first time that he should be directly associated, in the continuing tradition of English literature, with the seventeenth-century literary masters of learning and scientific inquiry, as well as with the dramatists. He is an amateur in science who gives expert dramatic illustration to the principles in Burton's professional scientific treatise. Melancholy is not Ford's only interest,[1] but it is a dominant one and is vital to a true comprehension of his work. For instance, the demonstration that Giovanni in *'Tis Pitty* is a victim of religious melancholy presents a totally new conception of this familiar figure

[1] See especially the studies by M. E. Cochnower, *Seventeenth Century Studies*; and by G. F. Sensabaugh, "John Ford and Platonic Love in the Court," *Studies in Philology*, XXXVI (1939), 206-26.

in the literature of the theatre; again, the analysis of Bassanes, the jealous husband in *The Broken Heart*, reveals how Ford uses melancholy to put new life into a stock character of the Elizabethan stage.

This study is not an application of the methods of the modern science of abnormal psychology to Ford's plays, or to Ford. It merely presents *The Anatomy* as the greatest repository up to its time of case histories and learned opinion in the field which we should now call abnormal psychology, and presents Ford as one who knew Burton's treatise well. The analysis is limited therefore, properly, I think, to terms and methods which will sound inexact and antiquated to a modern scientist, but which are the only ones Burton and Ford could have known. The attempt in summarizing *The Anatomy* has been to hold the spirit and effect of the original by using Burton's own turn of phrase as far as possible. I have not thought it necessary in this sort of condensation to mark all such phrases as quotations, since they are obviously Burton's and their source is duly indicated in the notes.

It is a pleasure to express my gratitude to Mr. Malcolm O. Young of the Princeton University Library, to Mr. Walter B. Briggs of Harvard College Library, and to Mr. H. A. C. Sturgess, Librarian and Keeper of the Records of the Middle Temple, London, for their courteous assistance; to Professor Willard Thorp of Princeton University and to Professor Gordon Hall Gerould, Editor of the Princeton Studies in English, for valuable suggestions; and especially to Professor Thomas Marc Parrott of Princeton University, who, through his encouragement, advice, and criticism, is responsible, directly or indirectly, for whatever excellence the study may have.

CONTENTS

x　　　　　　Contents

BURTONIAN MELANCHOLY

IN THE PLAYS OF JOHN FORD

I

AN EPITOME OF BURTON

DEFINITION

"MELANCHOLY" as used by Robert Burton in *The Anatomy of Melancholy* is the name of an aberration of the mind, "a chronick or continute disease,"[1] usually caused by neglect of bodily health and by excessive mental excitement. The outstanding symptoms are fear and sadness, without sufficient evident cause: "*a kind of dotage without a fever, having for his ordinary companions fear and sadness, without any apparent occasion.*"[2] It is difficult to cure but not incurable. If not inveterate, it usually yields to a treatment consisting of exercise, divertisement, sound advice, and, if possible, removal of the cause. "Melancholy" is thus simply a general term for mental disease. It includes all the neuroses and most of the psychoses treated by modern abnormal psychology.

The meaning of the word can be clarified if we begin by carefully distinguishing it from two other common interpretations: one, melancholy in the sense of mere romantic sadness; the other, melancholy in the sense of solemn meditation. Romantic melancholy is that transitory sadness which people experience at parting, or at an unpleasant revelation, or failure, or disappointment, or death. To take an example from the drama, it is the heartache that Philaster discloses when he hears of the supposed amour between his love Arethusa and his page boy Bellario (Euphrasia);[3] or the grief and self-reproach he expresses when in prison he comes to his senses after his

[1] Burton, I, 167. This and all following references to *The Anatomy of Melancholy* are to the edition of A. R. Shilleto, which is based on Burton's sixth edition, 1651. It should be observed that Burton revised his text for each new edition; but the changes after the third, 1628—the one which Ford presumably used—are immaterial.

[2] *ibid.*, I, 193.

[3] *Philaster*, III, i.

treasonous and ignoble attack upon Arethusa's life.[4] This is the general and accepted meaning in Ford's time and in our own. But it is the meaning which is especially to be guarded against in any intelligent discussion of Burton and Ford. Burton recognized it and termed it *"Melancholy in Disposition, improperly so called,"*[5] and definitely excluded it from his treatise:

> *Melancholy,* the subject of our present discourse, is either in disposition or habit. In disposition, is that transitory *Melancholy* which goes and comes upon every small occasion of sorrow, need, sickness, trouble, fear, grief, passion, or perturbation of the mind, any manner of care, discontent, or thought, which causeth anguish, dulness, heaviness, and vexation of spirit, any ways opposite to pleasure, mirth, joy, delight, causing frowardness in us, or a dislike. In which equivocal and improper sense, we call him melancholy, that is dull, sad, sour, lumpish, ill-disposed, solitary, any way moved, or displeased. And from these melancholy dispositions no man living is free, no *Stoick,* none so wise, none so happy, none so patient, so generous, so godly, so divine, that can vindicate himself. . . . But all these *melancholy* fits, howsoever pleasing at first, or displeasing, violent & tyrannizing over those whom they seize on for the time; yet these fits I say, or men affected, are but improperly so called, because they continue not, but come and go, as by some objects they are moved. This *Melancholy* of which we are to treat, is an habit, *morbus sonticus,* or *chronicus,* a chronick or continute disease, a settled humour, as *Aurelianus* and others call it, not errant, but fixed; and as it was long increasing, so, now being (pleasant or painful) grown to an habit, it will hardly be removed.[6]

The melancholy of Burton and Ford is to be distinguished also from solemn meditation, such as is invoked as the "goddess sage and holy" in the first few lines of *Il Penseroso.* The contrast is especially interesting in that this famous poem is exactly contemporaneous with what is presumably the period of Ford's greatest literary activity, and in that the initial idea and the metre of *Il Penseroso* have been traced[7] to the poem prefixed to Burton's *Anatomy of Melancholy,* entitled "The Author's

[4] *ibid.,* V, i.
[6] *ibid.,* I, 164, 167.
[5] Burton, I, 164.
[7] Hanford, p. 138.

Abstract of Melancholy." The hero of the poem does indeed present many of the symptoms of the Burtonian melancholic: his love of solitude,[8] his devotion to reading,[9] his preference for haunts which are woody and watered by a stream.[10] But to conclude from these facts that he is a melancholic is to make a point at the expense of the obvious intention of the poem. The hero, though not ever jubilant, leads a life of sober tastes, of composure and serenity; he is not distracted in mind or eccentric in action.

Burton's melancholy is to be distinguished in the other extreme from insanity or madness. Madness exceeds melancholy in degree: "far more violent than *melancholy*, full of anger and clamour, horrible looks, actions, gestures, troubling the patients with far greater vehemency both of body and mind"; madness exceeds melancholy also in kind: madness is "without all fear and sorrow":[11] the patient is beyond caring; he is unconscious of his illness. Melancholy unrelieved often passes into madness.

Burton distinguishes many other diseases of the mind which are forms of insanity rather than of melancholy: dotage, phrenzy, madness, hydrophobia, lycanthropia, St. Vitus' dance, ecstasy, etc. Of these the most important for our purpose are the following: Hydrophobia, a kind of madness which comes from the bite of a mad dog. Victims cannot endure the sight of water because they think that they see a mad dog in it, and they die rather than drink.[12] Lycanthropia, a form of madness in which men think themselves wolves, lie hid all day, and run barking and howling about graves in the night. There was, for example, "at *Alkmaar* in *Holland*, a poor husbandman that still hunted about graves, & kept in churchyards, of a pale, black, ugly, & fearful look."[13] St. Vitus' dance, so called because the victims are accustomed to go to St. Vitus for help; or "wanton melancholy" because they are not able to stop dancing. They dance over stools and tables, and great-bellied women have

8 *Il Penseroso*, ll. 77-92.
9 *ibid.*, ll. 97-120.
10 *ibid.*, ll. 131-46.
11 Burton, I, 160.
12 *ibid.*, I, 162-3.
13 *ibid.*, I, 161-2.

been known to dance until they fall exhausted and seem quite dead, yet never hurt their children.[14]

PARTS AFFECTED

The part of the body affected by melancholy, according to Burton and most writers, is the brain. But many other organs— the liver, the spleen, and especially the midriff and the heart —are involved, because they act in sympathy: they "have a fellow-feeling, by the law of nature: but forasmuch as this malady is caused by precedent *imagination,* . . . the *brain* must needs primarily be misaffected, as the seat of *reason*; and then the *heart,* as the seat of *affection.*"[15] The body is like a clock: if one wheel be loose, all the rest are thrown out of trim.[16]

KINDS

The kinds of melancholy are infinite.[17] They can be grouped for convenience in three classes "according to their seat": 1) head melancholy, which "proceeds from the sole fault of the brain"; 2) melancholy of the whole body; 3) hypochondriacal or windy melancholy,[18] in which *"the passage of the Chylus to the Liver is detained, stopped, or corrupted, and turned into rumbling and wind."*[19] Yet these classes, distinct in theory, are mixed in fact. Burton therefore first treats the whole subject generally in all its many manifestations, and reserves for special treatment at the end of his treatise three kinds distinguished by their principal causes: 1) love-melancholy, 2) jealous melancholy, 3) religious melancholy.

CAUSES

The causes are very numerous. The total number Burton lists, excluding duplication as far as possible, is more than eighty.[20] Nevertheless *"It is in vain to speak of cures, or think of remedies, until such time as we have considered of the causes."*[21] The cause may be a supernatural influence: from God himself, spirits, witches, or the stars. *"The constellation alone many*

---

14 *ibid.,* I, 163.
16 *ibid.* See also *ibid.,* I, 290.
18 *ibid.,* I, 200.
20 *ibid.,* I, 202-439.

15 *ibid.,* I, 195.
17 *ibid.,* I, 199.
19 *ibid.,* I, 436.
21 *ibid.,* I, 202.

times produceth melancholy, all other causes set apart,"[22] especially if Mars, Saturn, or Mercury be the planet of nativity.
For instance Saturn in baleful position produces a man "envi-
ous, covetous, jealous, and mistrustful; timorous, sordid, out-
wardly dissembling, sluggish, suspicious, stubborn; a contemner
of women, a liar, malicious, murmuring; never contented and
ever repining."[23] The natural cause of melancholy may be a
disproportion of the four humours. "A humour is a liquid or
fluent part of the body, comprehended in it, for the preservation
of it." There are four of them, named and characterized as
follows: 1) Blood: hot, moist, and red; 2) Pituita, or phlegm:
cold, moist, and white; 3) Choler: hot and dry; 4) Melancholy:
cold, dry, and black.[24] The correct proportion of these three
humours constitutes the "temperature" of the body; and excess,
or an "adustion,"[25] of any of them causes "distemperature."[26]
So frequently is an excess of the fourth humour, melancholy,
a principal cause of the distemperature, that the word *melancholy* has come to be accepted not only as the name of the
humour, but of the general distemperature of the body.

As the distemperature of the humours is the cause of the
disorder, so the distemperature in turn has its clear causes.
These causes are chiefly abuse of the six non-natural things.
"These six non-natural things are [1] diet, [2] retention, and
evacuation, which are more material than the other, because
they make new matter, or else are conversant in keeping or
expelling of it. The other four are [3] air, [4] exercise,
[5] sleeping, waking, and [6] perturbations of the mind, which
only alter the matter."[27] And chief among these six, both as
indicated by the elaborateness of Burton's discussion of them,
and by their applicability to our subject, are the fourth and
sixth.

"Nothing better than exercise (if opportunely used) for the
preservation of the body."[28] But overexercise refrigerates the

---

[22] *ibid.*, I, 236.   [23] Lilly, p. 36.
[24] Burton, I, 169-70.
[25] Scorching. An adust humour is "unnatural" and always causes trouble
whether it be in correct proportion or not. See Burton, I, 197-8.
[26] Burton, I, 432-4.   [27] *ibid.*, I, 248.
[28] *ibid.*, I, 277.

body, and stirs up and makes to rage the humours which Nature
would otherwise have concocted and expelled.[29] A deficiency
of exercise is equally bad; it is called "idleness (the badge of
gentry), . . . the bane of body and mind, . . . the chief author of all mischief, one of the seven deadly sins, and a sole
cause of this and many other maladies, the devil's cushion, as
Gualter calls it, his pillow and chief reposal."[30] Idleness will
produce melancholy in a man sooner than any other fault will
do it, in the opinion of one authority, and will insure its continuance. If he lives a life out of action, no doubt it makes
little difference; but if he does have duties, he will be unable
to perform them, even though they be necessary; he will be
unable to dress himself, to write a letter or the like.[31]

Concomitant with these physiological causes are a host of
mental causes, "passions and perturbations of the mind."[32]
Burton writes expansively on this subject and returns to it with
evident pleasure. For what is our life but *glucupricon*, a bitter
sweet passion, honey and gall mixt together? grudging and
complaint in the midst of mirth? For music we have the noise
of drums; for nuptial torches, the burning of towns; for
triumphs, lamentations; for joy, tears.[33] Joy will not come to
those who live beneath the moon; those who look for peaceable
and cheerful days, will find clouds, storms, calumnies.[34] In a
world of melancholy men, where philosophers and scholars,
critics, lovers, women,[35] are touched with this "sweet poison,"[36]
where indeed even kingdoms, animals, and vegetables[37] are not
free, Burton admits he too is "insane,"[38] and that it was to rid
himself of the malady that he wrote his treatise.[39]

The passions and perturbations of the mind can be divided
into two principal divisions: 1) love, joy, desire, 2) hatred,
sorrow, and fear.[40] In the first division belong ambition, that
gallant madness and pleasant poison, a dry thirst for honour;[41]

[29] *ibid.*, I, 277-8.
[30] *ibid.*, I, 278.
[31] *ibid.*, I, 279.
[32] *ibid.*, I, 287.
[33] *ibid.*, II, 147-8.
[34] *ibid.*, II, 149-50.
[35] *ibid.*, I, 126-30.
[36] *ibid.*, II, 121.
[37] *ibid.*, I, 86-7.
[38] *ibid.*, I, 137.
[39] *ibid.*, I, 18.
[40] *ibid.*, I, 297.
[41] *ibid.*, I, 324 ff.

covetousness, the desire of money (which is the root of all
evil) ;[42] love of pleasure—gambling, wine, and women;[43] love
of learning, the peculiar fury to which Robert Burton himself
is indebted. for the fame which brightens his name;[44] and,
finally, self-love, or vainglory, that delightful illusion which
is nourished on flattery,[45] or on the absence of it, as is the case
of the monk or hermit who decries all praise and honours and
is proud that he is not proud, who goes in simple clothes
whereas he could afford cloth of gold.[46] These loves, when
immoderate, are the fertile causes of melancholy and dotage.
In the second division (hatred, sorrow, and fear) belong envy,
which is sorrow for other men's goods and joy at their harms;[47]
anger, a cruel tempest of the mind, a temporary madness;[48] and
sorrow and fear. Sorrow holds the place of first importance
as "an inseparable companion, *the mother and daughter of
melancholy, her epitome, symptom, and chief cause*";[49] and
fear is rather another version of the same emotion than a
separate category, being an evil passion apprehended: "if present, it is sorrow; if to come, fear."[50] Allowing sorrow to be
the epitome of melancholy, we find it has as many manifestations as there are experiences of man. Some men suffer from
disgrace—particularly, generous men stung with the barbs of
public shame, whether it be trivial or great: a box on the ear
by an inferior, failure in the field, some foul fact committed
or disclosed.[51] A man may be a king, and appear to the casual
view most happy; yet he will prove to be in perpetual fear,
agony, suspicion, jealousy; and encumbered with cares.[52] Other
men are not content because they are confined, though they
have all else that could be wished: "sumptuous houses to their
use, fair walks and gardens, delicious bowers, galleries, good
fare & diet, & all things correspondent."[53] Yet others will not
be comforted as they mourn the loss of a dear one: a child,

[42] *ibid.*, I, 327 *ff.*
[44] *ibid.*, I, 348 *ff.*
[46] *ibid.*, I, 344-5.
[48] *ibid.*, I, 311 *ff.*
[50] *ibid.*, I, 297.
[52] *ibid.*, I, 321.

[43] *ibid.*, I, 332 *ff.*
[45] *ibid.*, I, 338 *ff.*
[47] *ibid.*, I, 305 *ff.*
[49] *ibid.*, I, 298.
[51] *ibid.*, I, 303.
[53] *ibid.*, I, 396.

a husband, or a friend;[54] and loss of honour, office, or good
name produces the same effect.[55]

The symptoms by which melancholy is to be recognized are
closely related to the causes, and often indeed partake of the
nature of the humour which is adust or in excess. Thus if the
disorder proceed from blood adust (hot, moist, and red), the
patient is given to laughter and witty discourse, is fond of
music, dancing, plays, and the company of women. The excess
of blood is evident in his countenance, which is ruddy in colour.
Democritus himself, the laughing philosopher, was such a man;
so was Sophocles, and many another philosopher, poet, or
prophet, for this kind of melancholy causes a divine ravish-
ment and a kind of divine inspiration.[56] If the disorder proceed
from phlegm adust (cold, moist, and white), the patient is
cold, slow, ass-like, sleepy, and delights in bodies of water. In
appearance he is pale or muddy of complexion and walks with
his eyes on the ground.[57] If the malady come from choler adust
(hot and dry), the victim is bold and impudent, ready to fight
but impatient to talk quietly. The choleric man is distinguished
from all other melancholy men by his readiness to endure tortures and death itself with courage and alacrity.[58] If the malady
arise from melancholy (cold, dry, and black), the patient is
cold and bashful, sad and solitary, fearful and suspicious. He
is apt to think of death and the grave and to imagine himself
to be dead. Night and blackness are the fitting setting for his
hallucinations, and his countenance itself is black or sallow.[59]
A mixture of these humours complicates the diagnosis, because
the symptoms are much confused. As is frequently the case,
Burton made little attempt to simplify or organize the evidence
of his authorities when speaking thus generally: instead he
resorted to direct quotation, not without perceiving and taking
advantage of the humorous effect thus produced.[60]

[54] *ibid.*, I, 414-15.
[55] *ibid.*, I, 416.
[56] *ibid.*, I, 460-1.
[57] *ibid.*, I, 459-60.
[58] *ibid.*, I, 461-2.
[59] *ibid.*, I, 462.
[60] For example, see Burton's quotation from Hippocrates and comment, I, 440.

On the other hand a classification of "signs in the mind" is easily to be made, even if Arculanús "will have these symptoms to be infinite":[61] the melancholy man is *fearful*. He fears that someone will kill him, that he will meet the Devil, that he will throw himself over a precipice if he come near it.[62] Such fears are *"without any apparent occasion"*;[63] equally groundless are those which attend him whenever he finds himself in a crowd of people, a situation which he particularly dislikes, as at a sermon: "if he be in a silent auditory, . . . he is afraid he shall speak aloud at unawares, some thing undecent, unfit to be said."[64] "He dare not come in company for fear he should be misused, disgraced, overshoot himself in gesture or speeches, or be sick; he thinks every man observes him, aims at him, derides him, owes him malice";[65] and all this in spite of the fact that melancholy men of this sort often have good memory, wit, and understanding.[66] The things that other people may say are equally terrifying: some cannot endure to hear the Devil named, or to see any tragical play, lest they be unable to get it out of their minds for days thereafter.[67] *Sorrowful.*[68] Sorrow is the "inseparable companion" as it is one of the invariable causes. In fact it is often the remembrance of some past disgrace, loss, injury, which returns ever and again as the fresh occasion for sadness. However, just as frequently it may be sorrow without a cause which afflicts the melancholy man the minute he wakes from a sleep which itself was troubled with terrible dreams. Finding it impossible to escape from his sorrow by any means, any more than a deer can run away from the fatal shaft which remains fixed in his side, his thoughts turn to death, and he frees himself from his insufferable torment by suicide. *Suspicious and jealous.*[69] By his distrust of everybody, even his closest friends, the melancholy man is limited utterly to his own resources; his self-consciousness is so increased that he can observe no event without applying it

[61] Burton, I, 442: "as indeed they are, varying according to the parties, *for scarce is there one of a thousand that dotes alike.*"
[62] *ibid.*, I, 444.
[63] *ibid.*, I, 193.
[64] *ibid.*, I, 444.
[65] *ibid.*, I, 445.
[66] *ibid.*, I, 441.
[67] *ibid.*, I, 446.
[68] *ibid.*, I, 447-9.
[69] *ibid.*, I, 449-50.

directly to himself. If he sees two men talking, whispering, or
jesting together, he thinks they discuss him; if they talk to
him, he interprets every word in its worst meaning. He cannot
endure to have any man look steadily at him, or even clear the
throat, point, or cough, without thinking he is ridiculed, contemned, or circumvented. *Inconstant.*[70] The melancholy man is
wavering and irresolute in mind and body, work and play. He
dislikes business of any sort, is unable to deliberate upon it
because of fear, and is persuaded to and fro by his counsellors.
He is always seeking change, having grown weary of each
place, each company, each book, each game, each mistress, in
turn. His judgment is good at one time, but at the next moment
it may be so perverted that he counts honesty dishonesty and
shows great solicitude for his enemy. *Humorous.*[71] The melancholy man is capricious: at one moment he may be extraor-
dinarily merry, and at another weeping without a cause, groan-
ing, sighing, pensive. Fantasy rules him awake as well as asleep.
The forms this fantasy may assume are, of course, innumerable.
The victim may conceive himself to be a dog, cock, horse, glass,
even a piece of butter who durst not sit in the sun for fear of
being melted.[72] Just as frequently the fantasy is projected from
the victim: goblins appear to him and talk; they are feared
but obeyed. Most frequently the fantasy is abstract and rests
on those causes which we have examined: the mind is tormented with an imagined and unreasoned fear or vexation.
Once he has entertained any of these conceits, he cannot be
rid of it, but against his will must think of it a thousand times
over. *Solitary.*[73] Like fear and sorrow, solitariness is a crown-
ing symptom and the natural result of all the foregoing symptoms. Melancholy is the affliction of the individual, not of the
social, man; hence he flees from his fellows to avoid conversation and to be alone with his anguish. Unfortunately he thus
cuts himself off from the most likely means of cure and insures
the continuance of the disorder. Circumstances may force him
to be content with confinement within his private house or
chamber, but if it is available, he prefers the secluded garden:

[70] *ibid.*, I, 450-2.   [71] *ibid.*, I, 452-3.
[72] *ibid.*, I, 463.   [73] *ibid.*, I, 454-5.

"they delight in floods & waters, desert[74] places, to walk alone in orchards, gardens, private walks, back-lanes, averse from company, as *Diogenes* in his tub."[75]

PROGNOSTICS

Melancholy is curable if taken early,[76] but incurable if inveterate.[77] "As *Job* was, they can neither eat, drink, or sleep: . . . they curse their stars with *Job, and day of their birth, and wish for death.*"[78] Hopeless cases thus usually end in suicide—"the greatest, most grievous calamity, and the misery of all miseries."[79]

CURE

The cure of melancholy may be effected by God. Next to Him, we must rely upon the physician, who is the Hand of God. The physician has three methods of cure at his disposal: pharmaceutical, chirurgical, and dietetical. An example of the first is the use of the mineral *granatus*, a kind of ruby found in Calicut, so named because of its resemblance to pomegranate seeds, which resists sorrow and recreates the heart when taken in drink.[80] An example of chirurgy is trepanning: " *'Tis not amiss to bore the skull with an instrument, to let out the fuliginous vapours. Sallust. Salvianus . . . saw a melancholy man at Rome, that by no remedies could be healed, but when by chance he was wounded in the head, and the skull broken, he was excellently cured.*"[81] The method of chief importance is dietetical, "which consists in reforming those six non-natural things,"[82] diet, evacuation, air, exercise, sleep, and perturbations of the mind. Among the six non-natural things our attention is most strongly directed to the third, fourth, fifth, and sixth.

Air. As the air is, so are the inhabitants, dull or witty, cleanly or clownish, sick or sound. "He therefore that loves his health, if his ability will give him leave, must often shift places, and make choice of such as are wholesome, pleasant, and convenient:

[74] Deserted.
[76] *ibid.*, I, 493.
[78] *ibid.*, I, 496.
[80] *ibid.*, II, 252.
[82] *ibid.*, II, 1.

[75] Burton, I, 455.
[77] *ibid.*, I, 494.
[79] *ibid.*, I, 495.
[81] *ibid.*, II, 280.

there is nothing better than change of Air in this Malady, and generally for health to wander up and down, as those *Tartari Zamolhenses*, that live in hordes, and take opportunity of times, places, seasons."[83] For peregrination charms our senses with unspeakable and sweet variety; he who has never travelled is a kind of prisoner, beholding from his cradle to his old age the same surroundings, still, still the same, the same.[84]

Exercise. Every man should have some regular employment. Riches cannot be had without labour, nor learning without study, nor health without bodily exercise.[85] The heavens themselves run continually around, the sun rises and sets, the moon increases and decreases, stars and planets keep their constant motions, the air is ever tossed by winds, the waters ebb and flow, to teach us that we should ever be in action.[86] The effect of exercise is to add strength to the entire body, to cleanse it by sweating, and to increase the natural heat by which food is digested; to spur the mind, to cure diseases, and to destroy vices.[87] Scores of kinds of exercises are recommended; familiar ones like tennis, hunting, hawking, riding, running, hurling, wrestling, and swimming; and less familiar ones: keelpins,[88] trunks,[89] mustering, baloon, riding of great horses, quintain,[90] and wild-goose chase. Walking is excellent, especially among orchards or gardens or woods, and near water;[91] so are dancing, singing, masking, mumming, and stage plays.[92] Exercise may be of the mind as well as of the body: visiting the inner rooms of sumptuous palaces, amid costly and beautiful furniture and decorations, sweet odours and exquisite music, with the company of gallant young men and fair virgins. It is refreshing to the soul to see fair-built cities, streets, theatres, temples; to observe some pageant, such as a coronation, a wedding, or the reception of a prince, with masques, shows, and fireworks; to see two kings in single combat or behold a battle fought.[93] Some people delight to hear, and some to tell, merry tales; all are

[83] *ibid.*, II, 71.   [84] *ibid.*, II, 78.
[85] *ibid.*, II, 81.   [86] *ibid.*, II, 80.
[87] *ibid.*, II, 82.   [88] Ninepins.
[89] A game resembling bagatelle. Also called "troll-madam." *OED.*
[90] Tilting.   [91] Burton, II, 83-6.
[92] *ibid.*, II, 97.   [93] *ibid.*, II, 87-9.

interested in the news: what the whole world is doing, what the Thracians, what the Chinese, and what is the latest scandal.[94]

But of all the recreations of the mind, none is so applicable to all men or so particularly suitable to expel melancholy as study. "Study delights old age, educates youth, adorns prosperity, is the solace and refuge of adversity, charms us at home, &c., find the rest in *Tully*."[95] Who is there so involved in worldly cares that he will not be much lightened in his mind by reading some enticing story, wherein as in a glass, he shall observe what our forefathers have done, the beginnings and ruins of nations, and private men's actions displayed to the life? Who is not earnestly affected with a passionate speech or an elegant poem? One may refresh his mind as well with studious pastimes other than the reading of books: what is so full of content as maps, pictures, statues, jewels, marbles; what is so pleasant as to view architecture, devices, coats of arms, old coins, artificial works, perspective glasses, and Roman antiquities?[96] Let the student, however, first be certain of the cause of his melancholy: "I can prescribe him no better remedy than this of study, . . . provided always that his malady proceed not from overmuch study, for in such cases he adds fuel to the fire."[97]

Sleep. Sleep is "the chiefest thing in all Physick,"[98] for it pacifies the mind and expels cares. If need be, it should be procured by medicines and protracted longer than ordinary as an especial help.

Perturbations of the mind. Correction of perturbations comes best of all from the patient himself, but he must desire, and must do his utmost for, his own good.[99] He thinks that every man observes him or laughs at him? It is fear and vain suspicion only; let him persuade himself so. He is sad, jealous, timorous? Let him examine the cause thoroughly; he will find there is no cause at all, or at most one that he will deride once he observes it. He can, if he will, master his affections.[100] Burton supplies a long consolatory digression at this point, containing

[94] *ibid.*, II, 93-4.
[96] *ibid.*, II, 100-1.
[98] *ibid.*, II, 114.
[100] *ibid.*, II, 122.

[95] *ibid.*, II, 100.
[97] *ibid.*, II, 107.
[99] *ibid.*, II, 119-20.

comforting ideas for all manner of particular discontents,
gleaned from the best authors. For instance, to such as are lame
or have other deformities and imperfections of the body, it may
be consolation to think that those imperfections "do not a whit
blemish the soul, or hinder the operations of it, but rather help
and much increase it."[101] After all, the best wine comes out of
old bottles, and many a famous man was ugly to look at.[102] But
if the patient's judgment be so depraved that he cannot seek his
own good, his next best course is to impart the troubles to a
discreet, trusty, loving friend; canker thrives on concealment.
Cure may come either from the mere telling[103] or from the
comfort, cheerful speeches, fair promises, counsel, and persuasion of the friend.[104] Music is often effective, for it has a quality
of divinity in it which extenuates fears, softens cruelty, brings
rest to the wakeful, and banishes hatred.[105] Mirth alone is a
principal engine to batter the walls of melancholy, a sufficient
cure, if it can be induced.

> By all means (saith *Mesue*) procure mirth to these men in
> such things as are heard, seen, tasted, or smelled, or any way
> perceived, and let them have all enticements, and fair promises,
> the sight of excellent beauties, attires, ornaments, delightsome
> passages, to distract their minds from fear and sorrow. . . .
> Let them use . . . a cup of good drink now and then, hear
> musick, and have such companions with whom they are espe-
> cially delighted; merry tales or toys, drinking, singing, dancing,
> and whatsoever else may procure mirth. . . . Beauty alone is
> a sovereign remedy against fear, grief, and all melancholy
> fits.[106]

In the most inveterate cases cure by deceit is not amiss: Alexander the Physician tells a story of a woman who thought she
had swallowed a serpent. He gave her a vomit, and conveyed
a serpent such as she imagined into the basin. As soon as she
saw it, she was cured.[107] If there be real cause of perturbation:

[101] *ibid.*, II, 154.
[102] Aesop, Socrates, Democritus, Horace, Melancthon, Galba the Emperor,
Epictetus, Alexander, Augustus. Burton, II, 155.
[103] *ibid.*, II, 123.
[104] *ibid.*, II, 129.
[105] *ibid.*, II, 133.
[106] *ibid.*, II, 138.
[107] *ibid.*, II, 131-2.

"No better way to satisfy than to remove the object, cause, occasion, if by any art or means possible we may find it out. If he grieve, stand in fear, be in suspicion, suspense, or any way molested, secure him, *solvitur malum*, give him satisfaction, the cure is ended; alter his course of life, there needs no other Physick."[108] As a last resort, if no other remedy will avail, it is sometimes possible to force out one nail with another, one grief or fear or passion with another, as they do nose bleeding by letting blood in the arm. Extreme examples are recorded, such as to pull out a tooth, to wound the patient or geld him, as they did epileptical patients of old.[109]

HEROICAL LOVE-MELANCHOLY

The best known book of *The Anatomy of Melancholy* is that which deals with love, which like any other passion or perturbation of the mind in excess, may cause melancholy.

> *Avicenna* . . . calleth this passion *Ilishi,* and defines it *to be a disease or melancholy vexation, or anguish of mind, in which a man continually meditates of the beauty, gesture, manners of his Mistress, and troubles himself about it: desiring* (as *Savanarola* adds) *with all intentions and eagerness of mind to compass or enjoy her, as commonly Hunters trouble themselves about their sports.* . . . *Arnoldus Villanovanus,* in his book of Heroical Love, defines it *a continual cogitation of that which he desires, with a confidence or hope of compassing it.*[110]

It is surprising that, although Ford is the dramatist of love and of melancholy, he draws only upon scattered parts of this book of *The Anatomy.* The following remarks merely group these ideas, without making a full analysis of the subject.

Among the allurements to love are the eyes and secret letters. The eye is the harbinger of love: it is the sluice which lets in soul-ravishing beauty and conveys it, sharper than any dart, directly to the heart.[111] And the eye is also the secret orator, the bawd of love: winks, glances, and private looks are like so many dialogues which bring lovers to understand each others'

---

[108] *ibid.*, II, 126-7.
[110] *ibid.*, III, 62-3.

[109] *ibid.*, II, 131.
[111] *ibid.*, III, 73.

meanings before they come to speak a word.[112] Secret letters
may accomplish the same thing.[113]

Among symptoms of love are the antithetical emotions it
produces in the lover: lovers may be sometimes almost rapt
beyond themselves for joy, yet for the most part love is a
plague, a hell. " 'Tis *suavis amarities, dolentia delectabilis,
hilare tormentum* [a sweet bitterness, a delicious pain, a gay
torment],"

> In love these vices are: suspicions,
> Peace, war, and impudence, detractions. . . .[114]

Love upsets a man's standards of judgment: "makes wise men
fools, so many times it makes *fools become wise*";[115] so that
he thinks his lady as beautiful as Venus even if she be de-
formed, wrinkled, pimpled, bald, blear-eyed, have rotten teeth,
a witch's beard, a sharp chin, a long crane's neck, filthy long
unpared nails, scabbed hands, a rotten carkass, a harsh voice,
incondite gestures, and a vile gait.[116] If the lover can get any
memento of his lady, such as a feather of her fan, her shoe-
string, or a curl of her hair, he will wear it in his hat or next
his heart. He adores her picture twice a day and stares at it
for two hours at a time.[117] He learns to play on a musical
instrument, makes rhymes in the lady's honour, and sings them
to her.[118]

The prognostics of love-melancholy are madness, murder,
and suicide. "He that runs head-long from the top of a rock, is
not in so bad a case, as he that falls into the gulf of love."[119]
But if the lover have his will and the two be married, the greatest happiness may be in store for him: "You know marriage
is honourable, a blessed calling, appointed by God himself in
Paradise, it breeds true peace, tranquillity, content and happiness, . . . [it] immortalises the human race. . . . No happiness is like unto it, no love so great as this of man and wife, no
such comfort, as *placens uxor*, a sweet wife."[120]

112 *ibid.*, III, 101.   113 *ibid.*, III, 117.
114 *ibid.*, III, 162-3. Translation is from the edition by Dell and Jordan-Smith,
p. 728.
115 *ibid.*, III, 197.   116 *ibid.*, III, 178.
117 *ibid.*, III, 192.   118 *ibid.*, III, 203-4.
119 *ibid.*, III, 214.   120 *ibid.*, III, 58.

JEALOUS MELANCHOLY

There are various kinds of jealousies improperly so called, such as that of parents, tutors, or guardians over their children or over those who are left in their wardship.[121] True jealousy is a branch of the mental disease which goes under our general word, melancholy, yet "so furious a passion"[122] that it may well be treated as a species apart, just as love-melancholy is treated. Indeed since there is *"No Love without a mixture of Jealousy,"*[123] it is perhaps a kind of love-melancholy. Love-melancholy usually goes before marriage, jealousy "doth usually follow, torture, and crucify in like sort."[124] Jealousy is defined as the fear that the lover has lest any foreigner should partici-pate with him in his love; or the fear that he should lose the affection of her on whom he is so much enamoured. When it has taken hold of the soul, it is "a main vexation, a most intolerable burden, a corrosive to all content, a frenzy, a madness itself."[125] Women are more jealous than men, by reason of the weakness of their sex.[126]

The principal cause of jealousy is incompatibility: an old man should not marry a young woman: old and young cattle do not plough well together;[127] persons unequal in fortunes and birth should not marry; and a sick, impotent person should not marry one who is sound, for the nuptial hopes are frustrated.[128] "Another main caution fit to be observed, is this, that though they be equal in years, birth, fortunes, and other conditions, yet they do not omit virtue and good education."[129] Before the ceremony is performed, let the betrothed consult an astrologer to see whether the significators in her horoscope agree with his, whether mutual love and duty or hate and domination be in store for them.[130] "My last caution is, that a woman do not bestow herself upon a fool, or an apparent melancholy per-

[121] *ibid.*, III, 296.
[123] *ibid.*
[125] *ibid.*, III, 303.
[127] *ibid.*, III, 346.
[129] *ibid.*, III, 349.

[122] *ibid.*, III, 295.
[124] *ibid.*
[126] *ibid.*, III, 305.
[128] *ibid.*, III, 347.
[130] *ibid.*, III, 356-7.

son":[131] "melancholy men are apt to be jealous, and jealous apt
to be melancholy."[132]

Then there are many things which increase a woman's desire
for other lovers and hence offer grounds for her husband's
suspicions. There are to be avoided: 1) the heat of southern
climates (Italy a paradise for horses, a hell for women) 2) impotency, if the man be old—cold and dry by nature; for if she
be "more craving, clamorous, unsatiable and prone to lust, than
is fit, he begins presently to suspect, that wherein he is defective,
. . . she will be pleased by some other means."[133] 3) Ugliness or
lack of grace in the man, especially if the woman be beautiful.
He has good grounds, for "beauty and honesty have ever been
at odds."[134] Even if she be not fair, yet "he holds it impossible
for any man living not to dote as he doth, to look on her, and not
lust, not to covet, and if he be in company with her, not to lay
siege to her honesty."[135] 4) Barrenness: if the wife cannot get
children by her husband, she will go elsewhere. Burton "could
give an instance, but be it as it is."[136] 5) Promiscuity before
marriage in men: "because they have been formerly naught
themselves, they think they may be so served by others, . . .
they shall have therefore *legem talionis* like for like."[137] 6) Opportunity: there are many men who will court, or tempt, or
compliment a likely lady to her undoing. They are to be found
in many places, and these of course the virtuous woman must
avoid: Plays, masques, feasts (for "in wine a woman knows
not her own husband"),[138] inns, the regions near stews or near
monasteries, wateringplaces, princes' courts, or places where
scholars have a frequent approach ("when a Scholar talks with
a maid, or another man's wife in private, it is presumed he saith
not a *Pater Noster.*")[139]

Symptoms of jealousy are like those of other kinds of melancholy, but much more violent. In appearance, the victim is given
to "strange gestures of staring, frowning, grinning, rolling of
eyes, menacing, ghastly looks, broken pace, interrupt, precipi-

[131] *ibid.*, III, 352.
[133] *ibid.*, III, 306.
[135] *ibid.*, III, 311.
[137] *ibid.*
[139] *ibid.*, III, 321.

[132] *ibid.*, III, 305.
[134] *ibid.*, III, 310.
[136] *ibid.*
[138] *ibid.*, III, 320.

tate, half-turns."[140] In mind, he is much tormented: listening to every whisper, applying it to himself, and amplifying its importance; changeable in his relations with his wife, at first cursing, threatening, brawling, scolding, fighting, and as soon again he will "flatter, and speak fair, ask forgiveness, kiss and coll, condemn his rashness and folly, vow, protest and swear he will never do so again."[141] His distracted mind also leads him to suspect his best friends and closest relatives: brother or sister, father or mother. "He thinks with those Italians,

> Chi non tocca parentado,
> Tocca mai e rado."[142]

A man in woman's clothes, a great chest, the back of a door, hangings, barrels, are objects of suspicion as hiding places. Windows close to the ground may yet be easily reached by rope ladders. He sets one servant to watch another, and all to observe his wife.

Prognostics of the disease are serious, for the usual course is from suspicion to hatred and from hatred to frenzy, madness, injury, murder or despair. The jealous man is as apt to maim or kill himself as to injure or murder the woman who has caused his sorrow. Sckenkius, for instance, "hath an example ... of a Baker that gelded himself to try his wife's honesty, &c. Such examples are too common."[143] And the cure resides in treatments which work through the mind: by a contrary passion, by counsel or persuasion (*"for a disease of the soul, if concealed, tortures and overturns it, and by no physick can sooner be removed than by a discreet man's comfortable speeches,"*)[144] by avoiding its onset (pare the nails before they grow long), by being always busy; and especially by being patient, for time will cure, age will bereave her of it. "There is no other cure. . . .

> The mind's affections Patience will appease,
> It passions kills, and healeth each disease."[145]

[140] *ibid.*, III, 322.   [141] *ibid.*
[142] *ibid.* Dell and Jordan-Smith, p. 841, translate:
      "Who doth it not in the family
        Is one who doth it never or seldomly."
[143] *ibid.*, III, 331.   [144] *ibid.*, III, 332.
[145] *ibid.*, III, 342.

RELIGIOUS MELANCHOLY

Religious melancholy may be of two sorts: 1) in excess, which is what afflicts men given to *"love to their own sect, hate of all other Religions, obstinacy, peevishness, ready to undergo any danger or cross for it; . . . blind zeal, blind obedience, fastings, vows, belief of incredibilities, impossibilities"*;[146] in a word, the melacholy of fanatics. 2) In defect. "Religious Melancholy in defect" in turn is of two sorts: 1) atheism, which is seen in men who are "secure, void of grace and fears,"[147] who do not believe "there is either Heaven or Hell, resurrection of the dead, pain, happiness, or world to come,"[148] and who laugh at others who do believe "for being such superstitious fools, to lose their lives and fortunes."[149] This disbelief in a future makes them Epicurean and hedonistic:

All their endeavours are to satisfy their lust and appetite, how to please their *Genius,* and to be merry for the present,

> Ede, lude, bibe, post mortem nulla voluptas.
> [Eat, drink, and love; all other things are naught.]

The same condition is of men and of beasts; as the one dieth, so dieth the other.[150]

Unless they repent, a time will come when they shall be called to account: they shall "certainly rue it in the end (*in se spuit, qui in coelum spuit*) their doom's at hand, and Hell is ready to receive them."[151] 2) despair, which is seen in people who have come to doubt that they are saved. No tongue can tell what pain and terror they experience. "There is no sickness, almost, but Physick provideth a remedy for it; to every sore Chirurgery will provide a salve: friendship helps poverty; hope of liberty easeth imprisonment; . . . authority and time wear away reproach: but what Physick, what Chirurgery, what wealth. favour, authority can relieve . . . a troubled conscience?"[152] Who can put to silence the voice of desperation? The prog-

146 *ibid.*, III, 397.   147 *ibid.*, III, viii.
148 *ibid.*, III, 434.   149 *ibid.*, III, 435.
150 *ibid.*   151 *ibid.*, III, 448.
152 *ibid.*, III, 463.

nostics of despair are extreme: utter torment, horrible blasphemy, violence, murder and suicide.

There are two principal kinds of atheists: 1)"Philosophers and Deists, who, though they be more temperate in this life, give many good moral precepts, . . . yet in effect they are the same (accounting no man a good Scholar that is not an Atheist) *nimis altum sapiunt, too much learning makes them mad,*" (i.e. melancholy).[153] A "philosopher" is then in the serious position of being melancholy by both disbelief and overstudy. In place of God they acknowledge Nature and Fortune as dictating the order of the world and of heaven.[154] The proof that no God exists rests upon such nice points as these: "*It cannot stand with God's goodness, protection and providence . . . to see and suffer one man to be lame, another mad, a third poor and miserable all the days of his life, a fourth grievously tormented with sickness and aches* to his last hour";[155] all therefore rests upon fate or chance; why else should kingship, wealth, honours, come to those who are wicked, base, unworthy?[156] They may seem to leave the question open, yet cavil with equal impiety: "*Si non sit Deus, unde bona? si sit Deus, unde mala?*"[157] 2)Libertines, "that impious and carnal crew of worldly-minded men, impenitent sinners, that go to Hell in a lethargy, or in a dream."[158] Such men may be professed Christians rather than professed atheists like those in the first class, but if so they "have cauterized consciences . . . *past all feeling, have given themselves over to wantoness, to work all manner of uncleanness even with greediness.*"[159]

"I have ended my task, and sufficiently illustrated that which I took upon me to demonstrate at first. At this present I have no more to say. *His sanam mentem Democritus,* I can but wish myself and them a good Physician, and all of us a better mind."[160]

[153] *ibid.*, III, 440.
[155] *ibid.*, III, 439-40.
[157] *ibid.*
[159] *ibid.*
[154] *ibid.*
[156] *ibid.*, III, 443.
[158] *ibid.*, III, 446.
[160] *ibid.*, I, 137.

II

MELANCHOLY IN THE PLAYS

CHRONOLOGY

TEN of Ford's plays are directly concerned with the theme of Burtonian melancholy: *The Witch of Edmonton, The Sun's Darling, The Lovers Melancholy, The Fancies, The Broken Heart, Loves Sacrifice, 'Tis Pitty, Perkin Warbeck, The Queen,* and *The Ladies Triall.* The chronology of these plays has been only tentatively established. To begin with, metrical evidence is confusing and contradictory. The results of the investigations of Hannemann,[1] Sherman,[2] and Pierce[3] are tabulated in the following diagram:

	% Feminine endings (Hannemann)	% Feminine endings (Pierce)	% Feminine endings in middle of verse (Hannemann)	Number of trisyllabic endings (Hannemann)	Number of trisyllabic endings (Pierce)	Number of rime-pairs (Sherman)	Number of rime-pairs (Hannemann)	Number of rime-pairs (Pierce)
Lovers Melancholy	38.4	36.7	.4	89	92	17	29	22
The Fancies	60.3	60.3	1.0	245	228	1	1	1
The Broken Heart	49.5	49.2	.7	206	187	20	19	21
Loves Sacrifice	14.9	14.9	.4	7	4	40	35	45
'Tis Pitty	13.8	14.9	.9	15	12	52	49	52
Perkin Warbeck	43.1	42.6	.6	146	148	10	11	11
Ladies Triall	43.7	41.7	.6	90	93	1	1	2

[1] *Metrische Untersuchungen.*　　　　　　　　[2] *Ford's Debt.*
[3] "The Sequence of Ford's Plays," *The Nation,* XCII (1911), 9-10.

It will be noticed that there is no consistent development in these plays when the use of feminine endings, the use of trisyllabic endings, and the use of rime are considered jointly. Neither are the plays consistently grouped by these talismans: for example *The Fancies* and *The Ladies Triall* are associated in the sparse use of rime, but completely unlike in the use of trisyllabic endings; *The Lovers Melancholy* and *Loves Sacrifice* are associated by the percentage of feminine endings occurring in the middle of a verse, but distinguished by the percentage of feminine endings as a whole. Only the two plays *Loves Sacrifice* and *'Tis Pitty* are consistently thrown together, but this fact does not throw any light on the proper position of the pair within the list.

Other internal evidence, such as topical allusions, is remarkably scarce, although the indefatigable Fleay has traced some out.[4] Judgments based on a study of developing poetic style, always subject to error, are especially dangerous in the case of Ford, for he was already a mature man (forty-two) and a veteran playwright, when he wrote the first play, *The Lovers Melancholy* (1628), with which this study is directly concerned. External evidence is fragmentary.

The chronology which is accepted as the foundation of this study is presented in the following table. The dates in Sir Henry Herbert's *Office-Book*, recording licenses for performance, are used in preference to all others, for it is a reasonable inference that most Stuart plays were licensed shortly after they were written. Lacking the license date, other conclusive external evidence is admitted. Failing the license date or other external evidence, entries in the *Stationers' Register* have been incorporated, not in the belief that they have any necessary connection with date of composition, but because they afford the most conservative positive evidence we have. In the absence of external evidence, pertinent internal evidence is admitted. As a last resort, the simple date of publication has been accepted. No play is moved from the position thus determined purely upon the basis of any critic's impressionistic judgment.[5] Only where evidence

---

[4] *Biographical Chronicle*, I, 230-5.
[5] For a digest of these judgments, see Sargeaunt, Chap. II.

is entirely lacking (*The Queen*) has personal opinion been the deciding factor. All dates are New Style.

Witch of Edmonton after Apr. 19, 1621	Before Dec. 29, 1621
The Sun's Darling	Before Mar. 3, 1624
The Lovers Melancholy	Before Nov. 24, 1628
The Fancies	Before Jan. 10, 1632?
The Broken Heart	Late 1632?
Loves Sacrifice	Before Jan. 21, 1633
'Tis Pitty	1633
Perkin Warbeck	Before Feb. 24, 1634
The Queen	1632-1634?
The Ladies Triall	Before May 3, 1638

The dates for *The Sun's Darling*,[6] *The Lovers Melancholy*,[7] and *The Ladies Triall*[8] are the dates of licenses for performance. The date *a quo* for *The Witch of Edmonton* rests on one of the facts of the case upon which the play was based: Mother Sawyer was executed April 19, 1621.[9] The date *ad quem* is the date of the first performance of which there is a record.[10] The dates of *Loves Sacrifice* and *Perkin Warbeck* are the dates of entry in the *Stationers' Register*. The date for *'Tis Pitty* rests solely upon the date of publication printed on the title-page. There is no evidence of any sort which will serve to date the composition of *The Queen*. Bang[11] judged from its style that it belongs near *The Broken Heart, Loves Sacrifice,* and *Perkin Warbeck*. There is at least no reason for preferring any other conjectural date than 1632-1634.

The date for *The Broken Heart* is an inference from three scraps of external evidence. The first occurs in a mock elegy written by William Hemming, son of Shakespeare's John Hemming, upon Thomas Randolph's finger, which was cut off in a tavern quarrel. This poem, which contains the much-quoted distich on Ford,

> Deep in a dump Jack Ford alone was got,
> With folded arms, and melancholy hat,

6 Adams, *Dramatic Records*, p. 27.
7 *ibid.*, p. 32.
8 *ibid.*, p. 37-8.
9 Bullen, I, lxxxi-cvii.
10 Murray, II, 193.
11 *The Queen*, p. viii.

is to be found complete only in a manuscript version in the Bodleian Library.[12] Hemming invites his grieved readers to behold the funeral pomp of the severed finger, with all the poets walking in procession behind the hearse. Each poet is then briefly characterized: Fletcher, Beaumont, Shakespeare, Massinger, Chapman, Daborne, Bartas, Quarles, May, Sandys, Digges, Daniel, Drayton, Wither, Browne, Shirley, Ford, Middleton, and Heywood. Hemming concludes his list with the remark,

> More worthies like to these I could impart,
> But that we are troubled with a Broken Heart.

The accepted date for the tavern quarrel is the latter half of the year 1632.[13] Since an elegy was normally written immediately after the death of its subject and since *The Broken Heart* is mentioned as if current on the stage, one infers that the play was written no later than the last months of 1632.

The second scrap of external evidence occurs on the title-page of the 1633 quarto, which reads, in part, "The Broken Heart. A Tragedy. Acted By the Kings Majesties Seruants at the priuate House in the Black-Friers." The only other Ford play acted by the King's Men, *The Lovers Melancholy,* appeared at both theatres, Globe and Blackfriars, as the title-page shows: "The Lovers Melancholy. Acted at the Private Hovse in the Blacke Friers, and publikely at the Globe by the Kings Maiesties Seruants." At this period the King's Men were accustomed to play at the Globe from May to November and at the Blackfriars from November to May.[14] The absence of a reference to the Globe on the title-page of *The Broken Heart* therefore indicates that the play had not been presented in the summer, and that its appearance in the winter was its first appearance. One thus infers that *The Broken Heart* was probably written no earlier than the summer of 1632.

[12] MS. Ashmole 38, reprinted by Parry in *Journal of English and Germanic Philology,* XIX (1920), 270-7. The poem was first published in 1656 in a much shorter form under the title "On the Time-Poets" in the collection of Cavalier poems called *Choyce Drollery.*

[13] See articles by Sidney Lee in *Dictionary of National Biography* and by Parry, *op. cit.,* p. 270.

[14] Adams, *Shakespearean Playhouses,* p. 225.

The third scrap of evidence is Crashaw's couplet,

> Thou cheat'st us, Ford; mak'st one seem two by art:
> What is Love's Sacrifice but the Broken Heart?[15]

which lends further support to the idea that *The Broken Heart* was composed before *Loves Sacrifice*. Otherwise the names of the plays would have been reversed.

The date for *The Fancies* is based upon the probability, first noted by Fleay,[16] that Shirley made sport of Ford and the play in his *Changes, or Love in a Maze,* which was licensed by Sir Henry Herbert on January 10, 1632.[17] Its sub-plot presents the antics of a group of Jonsonian "humorous" characters. There are two applicants for the hands of Chrysolina and Aurelia, the fair daughters of Goldsworth: Sir Gervase Simple, a rich country man just come up to town, and Caperwit, a conceited poet and fop, referred to as a "fresh innamorato,"[18] as "Democritus,"[19] and as "phantasma."[20] It is true that these epithets have a general application to the gallant conceited lover type. As Gerard (another rival lover) says, "the town is full Of these vain-glorious flashes,"[21] and the history of Cavalier poetry shows that Gerard was right. Nevertheless, the epithets fit exactly the popular report of Ford. One of the few contemporary comments on him which remain to us shows that the town accepted him as the typical inamorato,[22] and he had just made public acknowledgment, in *The Lovers Melancholy,* of his indebtedness to Democritus Junior (Burton).

Shirley was merry also at the expense of certain structural devices characteristic of Ford's plays. Caperwit considered a dance "the best language of some comedies," and knew that the gentlemen expected it "to be serv'd up in the middle."[23] Ford made extensive use of masques and dances, in the case of *The Lovers Melancholy* and *The Fancies* arranging the whole of the action around such a scene in the middle of the play.

---

[15] Bullen, I, lxxix.   [16] *Biographical Chronicle*, I, 234.
[17] Adams, *Dramatic Records*, p. 33.
[18] *Love in a Maze*, I, ii (Gifford and Dyce, II, 281).
[19] *ibid.*, III, i (Gifford and Dyce, II, 317).
[20] *ibid.*, V, ii (Gifford and Dyce, II, 353).
[21] *ibid.*, I, ii (Gifford and Dyce, II, 287).   [22] See above, p. 26.
[23] *Love in a Maze*, IV, ii (Gifford and Dyce, II, 339).

Next, *Love in a Maze* contained direct ridicule of the word
"fancy" as used by Ford. In Caperwit's estimation the first
quality to make a man a worthy lover is that he have "fancies,"
which he explains as being capable of "ravishing ladies." This
double entente is carefully repeated by the dramatist so that
nobody will miss it:

> *Cap.* What's he? [*Pointing to Sir Gervase*]
> *Golds.* A gentleman, that would endear himself.
> *Cap.* Has he any fancies in him? Can he ravish the ladies?
> *Golds.* Ravish ladies, sir? that's a dangerous matter.
> *Cap.* How many raptures does he talk a day?
> Is he transported with poetic rage?[24]

This curious use of "fancy" is unparalleled in contemporaneous
literature. It does not occur in Henry Cockeram's *The English
Dictionarie of 1623,* and its specialized meaning ("person
loved") is not referred to so early in *The Oxford English Dictionary.*[25] Even in other plays by Shirley the word has nothing
to do with "ravishing." In *The Gamester* (1633)[26] it is used as
a gambling term, meaning "streak of luck," "run"; and in *The
Example* (1634)[27] it is used in ordinary conversation to mean
"poetical inspiration," "conceit." The cant sense appears, then,
to be the particular property of Ford. "Fancies" he explains in
an ironical passage are "the pretty souls who are companions in
[Octavio's] house; all daughters to honest virtuous parents
and right worshipful; a kind of chaste collapsèd ladies."[28] The
play to which these ladies give their name revolves around the
mystery of their ostensibly improper relations with their pro-
tector, Octavio, a lascivious old man. Caperwit's use of "fancies" to mean "ravishing" therefore seems to mimic Ford.

Finally, Caperwit's self-description caricatures Ford:

> *Cap.* [*to Goldsworth*] Sir, I have a great ambition to be of
> your acquaintance. I hope you will excuse these fancies of

---

[24] *ibid.,* I, ii (Gifford and Dyce, II, 283).
[25] "Fancy-woman," meaning "a woman loved" or "a kept mistress," and
"fancy-man," meaning "a man loved" or "a man who lives upon the earnings of
a prostitute," are nineteenth-century expressions.
[26] *The Gamester,* III, iv (Gifford and Dyce, III, 240).
[27] *The Example,* V, iii (Gifford and Dyce, III, 363).
[28] *The Fancies,* II, ii (Bullen, II, 263).

mine; though I were born a poet, I will study to be your servant in prose: yet, if now and then my brains do sparkle, I
cannot help it, raptures will out, my motto is, *Quicquid cona-*
bor—the midwife wrapt my head up in a sheet of sir Philip
Sidney; that inspired me: and my nurse descended from old
Chaucer. My conversation has been among the Furies, and
if I meet you in Apollo, a pottle of the best ambrosia in the
house shall wait upon you.[29]

This applies point by point to Ford, and to no other contemporary so exactly. At the time it was spoken on the stage Ford
had just been giving public expression to a similar petulant
self-esteem in the Epilogue to *The Lovers Melancholy*:

> To be too confident is as unjust
> In any work as too much to distrust:
> Who from the laws of study have not swerv'd
> Know begg'd applauses never were deserv'd.
> We must submit to censure: so doth he
> Whose hours begot this issue; yet, being free,
> For his part, if he have not pleas'd you, then
> In this kind he'll not trouble you agen.[30]

His indebtedness to Sidney's *Arcadia* is well known,[31] all his
nurses use language even more indecent than dramatic custom
allowed,[32] and the dialogue of many of his characters is "among
the Furies."[33]

Now turning to the Prologue of *The Fancies*, evidently written at the time of publication, several curious and some unclear
statements therein take on meaning for the first time, and
corroborate the above conclusions:

> *The Fancies!* that's our Play; in it is showne
> Nothing, but what our *Author* knowes his *owne*
> Without a *learned theft*; no servant here

---

[29] *Love in a Maze*, I, ii (Gifford and Dyce, II, 284). *Quicquid conabor* is
evidently a fragment of *Quicquid conabar dicere, versus erat,* adapted by Sidney from Ovid, *Tristia* 4.10.26. See Cook's edition of Sidney's *The Defense of
Poesy*, Boston, 1898, p. 47 and note.

[30] Bullen, I, 106.   [31] See *Ford's Debt.*

[32] For instance, observe Kala in *The Lovers Melancholy*, III, ii (Bullen,
I, 54).

[33] For instance, observe the comic crew of *The Lovers Melancholy*, passim.

To some *faire Mistris*, borrowes for his eare,
His locke, his belt, his sword, the fancied grace
Of any pretty ribon; nor in place
Of charitable friendship, is brought in
A thriving *Gamester*, that doth chance to win
A lusty summe, while the good hand doth ply him,
And *Fancies*, this, or that, to him sits by him.
His free invention runnes but in conceit
Of meere imaginations: there's the hight
Of what *he* writes, which if traduc'd by some,
'Tis well (he sayes) he's farre enough from home.
For *you*, for *him*, for *us*, then this remaines;
Fancie, your [own] opinions, for our paines.[34]

Here Ford begins with his usual protest that his material is not
stolen from other authors, and states that he introduces no
thriving gamester who chances to win a big sum of money at
the sacrifice of friendship. (Shirley's *The Gamester* tells, among
other actions, the story of Hazard, the gamester who gives his
professional name to the play, and his unexpected success at
the tables, while his good friend Wilding loses.) *The Gamester*
would naturally have been in Ford's mind at the time, for it had
been printed some time after November 15, 1637,[35] just at the
time that *The Fancies* was being prepared for the press.[36] He
would naturally have chosen *The Gamester* for sarcastic reference because it had had the most brilliant success of all Shirley's
works: "The king sayd it was the best play he had seen for seven
years" when it was presented at Court on Thursday, February
6, 1634.[37] And that Ford is referring to Shirley's play is made
practically certain by the manner in which the name is printed:
both *Fancies* and *Gamester* are printed in italics and with capital
letters. If somebody maligns his play, Ford continues, that makes
no difference, for the maligner is so far away that his remarks
can scarce affect us. (Shirley was at this time in Ireland, whence

[34] Text from the reprint of the Quarto by de Vocht (Materials for the Study
of the Old English Drama, New Series, I, 250). The italics are Ford's.
[35] The date of its entry in the *Stationers' Register*.
[36] Printed some time after Feb. 3, 1638, the date of its entry in the *Stationers'
Register*.
[37] Quoted from Herbert's *Office-Book* by Nason, p. 74.

he did not return permanently until 1640.)[38] For him and for us, then, there remains the right to make up our own opinions of the play now presented for perusal.

Granting that this evidence shows that Shirley was writing an intentional satire of Ford and *The Fancies, The Fancies* could not have been written later than the season of 1631-1632.

The dates of *The Anatomy of Melancholy* are subject to no such uncertainty. The book was first published in 1621 and was reprinted in 1624, 1628, 1632, 1638, 1651, 1660, and 1676.[39] Thus the two decades of its greatest popularity coincide exactly with the two decades of Ford's greatest activity in the drama. He took the book up when it was new and not only became its outstanding exponent in the drama but continued to draw upon it all the rest of his life in the theatre. He wrote no play after *The Lovers Melancholy* (1628), if the canon of his plays as we have it is complete, that does not contain a study of a melancholy character.

THE LOVERS MELANCHOLY

The Lovers Melancholy is a tale of lovers' separation and reunion. Agenor, Prince of Cyprus, brings a beautiful lady, Eroclea, to his court, ostensibly to marry her to his son, Prince Palador. But Agenor himself attacks her, and she is forced to escape by flight from the country. He takes revenge upon her father, Meleander, by accusing him of treason, seizing his lands, and imprisoning him. The loss of Eroclea and the attendant distresses render melancholy both Palador and Meleander. At the same time Menaphon, unsuccessful suitor of the Princess Thamasta, leaves the court in despair and travels to Athens. There he chances to meet Eroclea, disguised for her protection as a page boy and called Parthenophil. They share each other's griefs, but Eroclea does not reveal her identity. After a year's exile they hear of the death of the wicked old prince and return to the court at Cyprus. Eroclea, still in disguise as a page boy, enters the service of Thamasta, who falls in love with "him."

[38] Nason, pp. 91-2, 117-18.
[39] *Dictionary of National Biography, s.v.* "Burton, Robert."

Menaphon is filled with anger and disgust at the supposed perfidy of the page boy and the dishonour of the princess.

Meanwhile the melancholy young Prince Palador has neglected affairs of state: the people are murmuring, the nobles are dissatisfied at the condition of the court, and the neighboring nations, long harassed by the injustices of the old prince, are on the point of attacking Cyprus. Sophronos, a counsellor of state, and Aretus, the prince's tutor, try to bring Palador to a realization of his danger, but fail. Observing that the prince is really ill, they put him in the hands of Corax, the court physician. Corax, a learned but bigoted professor at the university, undertakes by every treatment known to his science to cure the melancholy of Palador and Meleander. Every one fails. During this attempt he has to suffer the constant taunting of Rhetias, a malcontent courtier, who thinks all physicians are quacks. At length Corax and Rhetias compound their friendly quarrel for the general happiness, and Rhetias reveals the identity of Parthenophil. By this simple device Thamasta is restored to honour and to the love of Menaphon, Eroclea is reunited to her father and her lover, and the melancholy men are cured. Palador reinstates Meleander in his titles and properties, betrothes the lovers, and takes up firmly into his own hands the reins of government.

Prince Palador is the lover who is melancholy. In the first act, before he appears on the scene, his distraction is thoroughly described. Menaphon, just returned from Cyprus, asks if the court still wears the old looks, and Amethus answers him as follows:

> If thou meanest the prince,
> It does. He's the same melancholy man
> He was at's father's death; sometimes speaks sense,
> But seldom mirth; will smile, but seldom laugh;
> Will lend an ear to business, deal in none;
> Gaze upon revels, antic fopperies,
> But is not mov'd; will sparingly discourse,
> Hear music; but what most he takes delight in
> Are handsome pictures.[1]

[1] *The Lovers Melancholy*, I, i (Bullen, I, 12). The Burtonian sources of this passage and of a few others throughout this chapter were first specifically

Here are the symptoms from which a Burtonian physician could instantly recognize that the patient was melancholy: he is unduly sorrowful, irresolute in work and play, and taciturn. Ford is careful to exemplify this description in subsequent actions: Palador refuses to deal in business in Act II, Scene i; he indulges his taste for revels, antic fopperies, and music when he attends Corax's "strange masque"[2] (III, iii); the delight in handsome pictures apparently is illustrated by the admiration he bestows upon the "tablet" of Eroclea he carries over his heart (II, i), a picture so excellent that her father thinks "the cunning arts-man Falter'd not in a line."[3] There is no scene, however, in which he does not "speak sense."

The prince's appearances on the scene are infrequent—only twice in the course of the first three acts—for love of solitude is characteristic of a melancholy man. As soon as he does appear (II, i), we observe additional symptoms. He shows himself "averse from company" by an ill-tempered question as the only reply to the obeisance of his courtiers: "Why all this company?"[4] The physician Corax, ignoring the remark, takes the prince roughly to task for his failure in the fourth of the six non-natural things, exercise:

> A book! is this the early exercise
> I did prescribe? instead of following health,
> Which all men covet, you pursue disease.
> Where's your great horse, your hounds, your set at tennis,
> Your balloon-ball, the practice of your dancing,
> Your casting of the sledge, or learning how
> To toss a pike? all chang'd into a sonnet![5]

The particular exercises Corax has suggested and Palador has not undertaken show a close reading of Burton's suggestions for cure. Corax also condemns the young prince for writing sonnets, perhaps because he thinks the prince is suffering from "heroical love-melancholy." Making love-rhymes is a symptom of it. As a matter of fact, Palador does not write sonnets, as

pointed out by M. E. Cochnower in "John Ford," *Seventeenth Century Studies.*

2 *ibid.*, IV, iii (Bullen, I, 82).   3 *ibid.*, V, i (Bullen, I, 99).
4 *ibid.*, II, i (Bullen, I, 31).   5 *ibid.*

far as we know. Nor is he a learned man, although he inadvisedly carries a book with him into the audience chamber. Melancholy can be caused by excessive love of learning, but his book is not a symbol of habitual application to study; it is rather a point of departure for Corax's disapproval and the objectification of Palador's disobedience. Corax concludes with a threat to desert the service of his prince and return to the university, even if it mean the loss of his head:

> 'twere better
> For me to lose it than to lose my wits,
> And live in Bedlam; you will force me to't;
> I'm almost mad already.[6]

Palador answers with the inconstancy and occasional wit of the melancholic: "I believe it." Unimpressed by a recital of serious danger to the peace and honour of his country, he shows the suspicion of the melancholy man when he is told that his subjects talk of him. Fearing that he is ridiculed, contemned, or circumvented, he "borrows patience" to hear each of the courtiers in turn say how he is "interpreted."[7]

The prince's most hoary advisor, Sophronos, speaks first. He has the specialized knowledge of Burton which one would expect from Corax or perhaps Aretus. He condemns the prince's inconstancy; he testifies to Palador's habit of following his own inclinations, and, by implication, to his neglect of affairs of state—duties which are necessary but which Palador is unable to perform:

> Not willingly provok'd, but withal headstrong
> In any passion that misleads your judgment:
> I think you too indulgent to such motions
> As spring out of your own affections.[8]

Out of the depth of his years of experience in statecraft he adds what is at once a summary of the situation and a prophecy of despair:

> Too old to be reform'd, and yet too young
> To take fit counsel from yourself of what
> Is most amiss.[9]

[6] *ibid.*
[8] *ibid.*

[7] *ibid.* (Bullen, I, 32).
[9] *ibid.*

Aretus's observation is the same: the prince is intent on his
pleasure to the detriment of affairs of state; but in addition he
is the victim of vainglory, which is a cause of melancholy:

> I think you dote—with pardon let me speak it—
> Too much upon your pleasures; and these pleasures
> Are so wrapt up in self-love, that you covet
> No other change of fortune; would be still
> What your birth makes you; but are loth to toil
> In such affairs of state as break your sleeps.[10]

This severe arraignment is corroborated by Corax in a speech
even more "plain and brief,"[11] than Sophronos's. Palador
receives with indifference the opinion of these who should be his
most trusted advisors, but listens seriously to the words of
Rhetias, a known malcontent of the court and presumably not
one of Palador's well-wishers. When all the other courtiers
have "stol'n hence,"[12] the prince confides in Rhetias the secret
cause of his melancholy—the loss of Eroclea; yet he fears that
even this new friend may be an enemy, and that he is being
left out of councils and ridiculed behind his back: "I know
thou wert put on to sift me."[13] No sooner have the courtiers
returned than Palador's aversion to company reasserts itself:
he answers with short and ungracious phrases the proffered
duties of Menaphon (who has been absent for a year)[14] and
of Parthenophil (a total stranger). Thamasta, eager to tell the
romantic story of Parthenophil's "first acquaintance" is silenced
with a cold "Some other time";[15] and Palador escapes back to
his melancholy solitude.

Palador, then, is a victim of melancholy, but it is not heroical
love-melancholy, even though he is a lover; for in love-melancholy the mistress is alive and present and the lover's ailment
is that he desires with all intentions and eagerness of mind to
compass and enjoy her. Palador rather is furnished with a wealth
of symptoms of general melancholy, drawn from the body of
The Anatomy, not from the section dealing with Heroical Love-

---

[10] *ibid.* (Bullen, I, 32-3).   [11] *ibid.* (Bullen, I, 32).
[12] *ibid.* (Bullen, I, 34).   [13] *ibid.* (Bullen, I, 37).
[14] *ibid.,* I, i (Bullen, I, 11):
    "Twelve months we have been sunder'd."
[15] *ibid.,* II, i (Bullen, I, 39).

Melancholy. His affliction described in terms of its cause could best be called melancholy resulting from the loss (as he believes) of a dear one and from the public disgrace suffered by his family.

Having thus presented the melancholy problem in word and action in the first two acts, Ford is ready for its solution. He creates two agencies for this purpose: supposedly expert scientific treatment by Corax, very inexpert but humanly sympathetic treatment by Rhetias. Each of these characters is allowed a generous portion of the time of the play for carrying out his plans. Corax's specialized knowledge is first demonstrated. Sophronos and Aretus, having already despaired of helping the prince by friendly advice in Act II, Scene i, and having agreed to call in the assistance of Corax, engage him in a discussion of the malady in Act III, Scene i:

> *Soph.* We find him timely now; let's learn the cause.
> *Are.* 'Tis fit we should.[16]

And Aretus proceeds to a leading question on the physiological causes of melancholy:

> Since your skill can best discern the humours
> That are predominant in bodies subject
> To alteration, tell us, pray, what devil
> This melancholy is.[17]

But Corax is of the opposite opinion that "Melancholy Is not, as *you* conceive, indisposition Of body, but the mind's disease,"[18] for which, be it granted, he has the authority of most writers quoted by Burton. Its several kinds, he continues, are "Ecstasy, Fantastic Dotage, Madness, Frenzy, Rapture[19] Of mere imagination." Burton distinguished these forms of madness (not melancholy) very precisely, but in *The Lovers Melancholy,* he is the acknowledged basis[20] only for a very colorless and

---

[16] *ibid.*, III, i (Bullen, I, 52).

[18] *ibid.* Italics mine.

[17] *ibid.*

[19] Quarto reads "Rupture," which is preferable. There is, however, no definition for either rapture or rupture of the imagination in *The Anatomy.* The phrase is probably original with Ford.

[20] This is the passage to which Ford wrote the footnote, "Vide *Democritus Junior.*"

gratuitous statement from Corax that they "differ partly From Melancholy."[21] Corax makes better use of his foundation when he says melancholy is

> A mere commotion of the mind, o'ercharg'd
> With fear and sorrow; first begot i' th' brain,
> The seat of reason, and from thence deriv'd
> As suddenly into the heart, the seat
> Of our affection.[22]

Aretus, a good tutor if only in his ability to ask repeated questions, turns back then to kinds of melancholy; to which Corax replies, with Burton, the kinds and causes are infinite in number. Sophronos asks if Corax thus concludes that since the cause is doubtful, the cure will be impossible. It is true according to medicine from Galen to Burton that it is in vain to speak of cures until we have considered of the causes, but Sophronos has not heard Corax say so. Corax's answer is brisk: "My lord, you are too quick: thus much I dare Promise and do; ere many minutes pass I will discover whence his sadness is, Or undergo the censure of my ignorance."[23] He refers to his attempt at cure, the "scholar's fancy"[24] he presents with the assistance of all the comic characters of the play (and some others who are not named), his "Masque of Melancholy." We are to expect nothing but sadness in this masque, then, asks the prince's tutor. Madness, rather, answers Corax, for

>   Melancholy is
> The root as well of every apish frenzy,
> Laughter, and mirth, as dullness.[25]

This is Burton's distinction between true melancholy and melancholy in disposition only.

The masque (III, iii) makes double use of Burton: 1) in substance it is a dramatization of diseases he discusses; 2) in purpose it is an application of his therapeutic principle that melancholy can be cured by diversion. The diseases presented in the masque are lycanthropia, played by Rhetias; hydrophobia, played by Pelias; delirium, played by "a Philosopher"; phrenitis,

---

[21] *The Lovers Melancholy*, III, i (Bullen, I, 52).
[22] *ibid*. (Bullen, I, 52-3).   [23] *ibid*. (Bullen, I, 53).
[24] *ibid*., III, iii (Bullen, I, 63).   [25] *ibid*. (Bullen, I, 63-4).

played by Grilla; hypochondria, played by Cuculus; wanton melancholy (or St. Vitus' dance), played by "a Sea-Nymph." Gifford thought these characters were produced with very little inspiration and preferred to read them in Burton's pages.[26] And indeed there is a perfect confusion of symptoms: suspicion of one's wife's honesty, which Pelias shows, has no relation to hypochondria; ambition and self-love are not causes of delirium; phrenitis is not caused by pride and it does not "reign most in women"; over-curiosity, loss of goods, loss of friends do not cause hypochondriacal melancholy, while fear and sorrow do so only according to some authorities. I can see no method in this mad confusion unless it be a clumsy jibe at Corax. Damned as a quack and imposter,[27] ridiculed by Rhetias whenever they appear together,[28] and unsuccessful in his practice, Corax is here allowed to make a fool of himself by getting mixed up in his own science. For if we view the masque as a performance on the stage rather than as a scene in Gifford's study, and observe the masquers' costumes, speeches, and actions, we find all the consistency which is lacking in Corax's tags and comments. Rhetias is painted and dressed in the fashion of an actual person who suffered from lycanthropia; he says he is "turned wolf" and accordingly he barks; and now that it is midnight, he goes to a churchyard; here he gruesomely tears off "a piece of raw meat" at which he gnaws and growls "arre." This certainly is lycanthropia. Pelias is dressed in a crown of feathers and recalls the days when as emperor his hand was kissed. At the same time he is obsessed with the idea that his wife cuckolds him. And third, since he was bitten by a mad dog, he fears water and provides that it shall be treason to wash or even to mention water throughout all his dominions. His affliction is triple: delusions, jealous melancholy, hydrophobia. (Corax allows that it is hydrophobia "mix'd with jealousy.") The philosopher is dressed in black rags and an old gown half off, for he is very, very poor. But he is proud of being an intellectualist: his opinions are pure and perfect, and opinion rules the

[26] Bullen, I, 63, n. 16.
[27] *The Lovers Melancholy*, I, ii (Bullen, I, 22, 23).
[28] *ibid.* (Bullen, I, 22-4); IV, ii (Bullen, I, 73-4).

world. This is actually an illustration of the malady which
afflicts those vainglorious hermits who are proud that they are
not proud, who go in simple clothes whereas they could afford
cloth of gold. Corax is consistent in mentioning ambition, sin-
gularity, self-love, and "blind opinion of true merit" as causes.
But the malady is certainly not delirium (a disease which Burton
does not treat) as Corax says, much less dotage (which is merely
a synonym for melancholy generally) as Gifford stupidly indicates.[29] Grilla is pranked out in ridiculous finery with fan and
muff, and apes the manner of a great lady kissing her lapdog.
This is mere pride, which Corax mentions as one of the causes,
but it has no relation to phrenitis. Cuculus is dressed like a
Bedlam, which is to say simply like a madman. He sings of
rumbling and gives a practical and vulgar demonstration of
what happens when "a windy flatuous humour" seeks vent from
"the animal parts."[30] This is certainly hypochondria. And
finally, the Sea-Nymph is "big-bellied" and madly dances. This
"strange fury" is St. Vitus' dance or "wanton melancholy," as
Corax says, recalling the Burton legend about pregnant women:

> Women
> With child, possess'd with this strange fury, often
> Have danc'd three days together without ceasing.[31]

Palador observes the masque calmly enough even in the
presence of Parthenophil, who embodies what Corax thinks is
the prince's own disease, love-melancholy. But when Corax
uses the word "devil," Palador interrupts with vehemence. As
we know, many a melancholy man cannot endure to hear the
Devil named. With a few muttered excuses Palador flees from
the hall in terror and returns a second time to his melancholy
solitude. Rhetias has allowed Corax free rein in the attempt to
cure the prince with the masque. The plan has met with a
qualified success: whereas the prince is not cured of his melancholy, he is at least disturbed. Everybody in the court observes
the change that has come over him: Sophronos: "I never saw

[29] Bullen, I, 65, n. 19.
[30] His exclamation, "Bounce!" is one of the Elizabethan cant words for
breaking wind.
[31] *The Lovers Melancholy*, III, iii (Bullen, I, 68).

him So much distemper'd"; Aretus: "The prince is throughly
mov'd."[32] We realize that this circumstance is not a favorable
sign and that Corax has only made matters worse when the
prince speaks his own mind—now he is nearly mad, now

> the very soul of reason
> Is troubled in me:—the physician
> Presented a strange masque, the view of it
> Puzzled my understanding.[33]

It is therefore Rhetias's turn to try his hand. His regimen
is as simple and human as Corax's was elaborate and scientific.
By being blunt and honest, and by testing the prince with a
well-turned story of the events of the last two years (II, i), his
assurance that he can cure the melancholy prince is already firm
even before Corax's masque is presented. Palador, thanking him
later, says (referring to Act II, Scene i):

> O, Rhetias, thou art just; the youth thou told'st me
> That liv'd at Athens is return'd at last
> To her own fortunes and contracted love,

and Rhetias admits "My knowledge made me sure of my report,
sir."[34] What he knew was the cause of Palador's distemper:
the loss of Eroclea; that, and no more. The cure is equally
simple: remove the cause, give him satisfaction, restore Eroclea
to his arms. No wonder it is that Rhetias exults over Corax:
"O these lousy close-stool empirics, that will undertake all cures,
yet know not the causes of any disease!"[35] His confidence is
justified in Act IV, Scene iii, where Eroclea is presented in a
"double disguise" made possible by the confused state of the
prince's mind: for some time Palador is afraid to believe that
Eroclea has returned alive, and thinks he sees only the boy who
played the rôle of love-melancholy in Corax's masque dressed
in the clothes of Eroclea. This device, sometimes called "retro-
disguise," has occurred only very infrequently in the Elizabethan drama.[36] Palador's doubt is soon dispelled, and the scene

---

[32] *ibid.*, IV, iii (Bullen, I, 81). [33] *ibid.* (Bullen, I, 82).
[34] *ibid.*, V, i (Bullen, I, 94). [35] *ibid.*, IV, ii (Bullen, I, 73).
[36] See Freeburg, pp. 11-12, 80-3.

closes on a note of peace as richly harmonious as any to be found
in the work of him

> whose hand with high funereal art
> Carved night, and chiselled shadow,[37]

when Palador says

> We are but fools
> To trifle in disputes, or vainly struggle
> With that eternal mercy which protects us.
> Come home, home to my heart, thou banish'd peace![38]

Rhetias's cure has succeeded in an instant where the learning
and prolonged labours of Corax struggled in vain.

"The fame of our young melancholy prince," said Menaphon
in the opening scene of *The Lovers Melancholy* was the first
report which prevailed upon Parthenophil to accompany him
back to Cyprus. Another was "Meleander's rare distractions."[39]
The clue to Meleander's particular kind of melancholy is given
early (II, ii) by Trollio, the old man's faithful servant:

> *Mel.* Am I stark mad?
> *Trol.* [*aside*] No, no, you are but a little staring; there's dif-
> ference between staring and stark mad. You are but whimsied
> yet; crotcheted, conundrumed, or so.[40]

These crotchets and whimsies are the fantasies which come to
plague the melancholy man in his symptom of humorousness.
One need not go beyond Burton's discussion of humorousness
to find all the rest of his melancholy symptoms: he groans
"humorously" off-stage immediately before his first appearance, and Trollio's remark, though jesting, shows how much
importance is to be attached to this symptom:

> *Cleo.* Dost hear that groan?
> *Trol.* Hear it! I shudder: it was a strong blast, young mis-
> tress, able to root up heart, liver, lungs, and all.[41]

No sooner has the arras been drawn away and Meleander wak-
ened from his sleep than his mind turns "humorously" back to

---

[37] Swinburne, *Sonnet: John Ford.*
[38] *The Lovers Melancholy*, IV, iii (Bullen, I, 86-7).
[39] *ibid.*, I, i (Bullen, I, 16).   [40] *ibid.*, II, ii (Bullen, I, 44).
[41] *ibid.* (Bullen, I, 42).

memory of his grief, the loss of his daughter. The public disgrace of Eroclea, who was all purity, tortures his memory as well as the fact that she is now dead, as he believes:

> Yet, when winds and storm
> Drive dirt and dust on banks of spotless snow,
> The purest whiteness is no such defence
> Against the sullying foulness of that fury.
> So rav'd Agenor, that great man, mischief
> Against the girl.[42]

His wrath against the family of Agenor includes even Agenor's nephew Amethus, who desires the hand of Cleophila, and all the courtiers,[43] and swings back again to the death of Eroclea; against his will he must think of it a thousand times over. A "humorous" laugh with wormwood in it greets Rhetias's affectionate submission to Meleander's commands. Meleander is a victim, then, of melancholy caused by the loss of his honours to corrupt courtiers, by public disgrace inflicted upon his daughter and his family, and by the loss of Eroclea.

In a more violent mood in Act IV, Scene ii, which opens in the comic vein and quickly alters to the pathetic, Meleander is still showing signs of humorousness: instead of fancying himself a dog, cock, bear, horse, or butter, he is acting the rôle of a lion. He thunders, every word which comes out of his mouth roars like a cannon, once he shook the house with his roar. Trollio is so afraid of him that he has provided himself with a "morion"[44] for his protection. After a preliminary roar off-stage (as he had groaned before) he enters with this leonine challenge:

> Show me the dog whose triple-throated noise
> Hath rous'd a lion from his uncouth den
> To tear the cur in pieces.[45]

Calmed when Corax greets him in kind, his mind reverts as usual to the evils of court practice, wriggling in to rooms of state, and the loss of Eroclea. When the talk turns to gallows

[42] *ibid.* (Bullen, I, 44).
[43] *ibid.* (Bullen, I, 45-6).
[44] Helmet.
[45] *The Lovers Melancholy*, IV, ii (Bullen, I, 75).

and the hangman, Corax diverts Meleander by pretending that he too has a daughter to whom he wants to bid farewell before they hang each other. The trick causes Meleander intense suffering. As he reproaches Corax, he reveals that sometimes his melancholy has gone over into true madness: when he is frantic, he is free of fear and sadness; only when he is reclaimed to reality, are his griefs struck home:

> Cruel man!
> How canst thou rip a heart that's cleft already
> With injuries of time?—Whilst I am frantic,
> Whilst throngs of rude divisions huddle on,
> And do disrank my brains from peace and sleep.
> So long—I am insensible of cares.
> As balls of wildfire may be safely touch'd,
> Not violently sunder'd and thrown up;
> So my distemper'd thoughts rest in their rage,
> Not hurried in the air of repetition,
> Or memory of my misfortunes past:
> Then are my griefs struck home, when they're reclaim'd
> To their own pity of themselves.[46]

The treatment of Meleander, like that of Palador, is undertaken in two scenes: in one (IV, ii) Corax tries the elaborate methods of science; in the other (V, i) Rhetias and Corax combine their forces in a very simple method. In Act IV, Scene ii, Corax has diagnosed the old man's ailment, and delivers his verdict with the patronizing manner he always assumes with Rhetias:

> 'Tis not a madness, but his sorrows—
> Close-griping grief and anguish of the soul—
> That torture him; he carries hell on earth
> Within his bosom: 'twas a prince's tyranny
> Caus'd his distraction; and a prince's sweetness
> Must qualify that tempest of his mind.[47]

But as yet Corax does not have the means to "a prince's sweetness," so he must use his old bag of tricks; hence the remainder of the scene. Corax tries in several ways to ameliorate the old man's distress by Burtonian deceits, all of them applications

46 *ibid.* (Bullen, I, 77).   47 *ibid.* (Bullen, I, 73-4).

The Lovers Melancholy   45

of the advice to force out one nail with another. Does Meleander
roar like a lion? Corax meets him with a fearful mask and
threatens to crush his bones and puff him into air. Does Meleander think the scaffold a better cure for melancholy than
"all The buzz of drugs and minerals and simples, Bloodlettings,
vomits, purges"—Burton's pharmaceutical treatment—? Corax
will be the first candidate:

> Fix the knot
> Right under the left ear.[48]

Does the old man think of Eroclea? The physician tells the
story of her life as if she were his own daughter. Yet the cure
does not succeed: the scene ends with the old man's mind more
indelibly than ever on the loss of Eroclea. Cardenes in Massinger's *Very Woman* was afflicted with a melancholy caused
by injustices similar to those which distress Meleander; but the
deceits which cured him have no effect on Meleander.[49] Yet
Paulo is no more of a physician than Corax. The vital difference
between the treatment of the two plays is that Ford recognizes,
with Burton, that a mental ailment such as Meleander's is too
deep for such cure:

> Fool, the weight
> Of my disease sits on my heart so heavy,
> That all the hands of art cannot remove
> One grain, to ease my grief.[50]

In Act V, Scene i, Corax's scientific treatment is still continuing: he has given the old man a drugged drink to induce
a long sleep, "the chiefest thing in all Physick," and calls him
back to consciousness with a beautiful song, for music has a
quality of divinity in it which extenuates fears. But it is still
not these means that restore Meleander to happiness. Rather
the cure of his melancholy is effected by the removal of its
causes, in which Corax and Rhetias combine: restoration of
his honours and addition to them—Marshalship of Cyprus,
Commandership of the Ports; reconciliation with the formerly

---

[48] *ibid.* (Bullen, I, 76).
[49] Gifford noted the parallel (Bullen, I, 105, n. 17).
[50] *The Lovers Melancholy*, V, i (Bullen, I, 97).

maleficent royal house; and, above all, the return of his lost daughter—"to behold Eroclea safe will make him young again,"[51] as Palador puts it.

Palador and Meleander are the central figures in this story of melancholy, and their affliction imperils the health of the great families of which they are the heads. Another character catches it from them: Menaphon is touched lightly with the "sweet poison": it was to disburden himself of "discontents" that he travelled abroad, only to find "the grief Is still the same"[52] upon his return. And stung with the disgrace of the princess, he determines to cultivate his affliction:

> Henceforth I will bury
> Unmanly passion in perpetual silence:
> I'll court mine own distraction, dote on folly,
> Creep to the mirth and madness of the age,
> Rather than be so slav'd again to woman.[53]

As a direct result of Palador's affliction the kingdom also becomes melancholy, as Burton said one might. Corax damns the court for a madhouse,[54] Sophronos laments the sickness of the court and commonwealth,[55] while Rhetias finds the commonwealth and the times themselves out of joint:

> I will not court the madness of the times;
> Nor fawn upon the riots that embalm
> Our wanton gentry.   .   .   .
>   .   .   .   When commonwealths
> Totter and reel from that nobility
> And ancient virtue which renowns the great,
>
> .   .   .   .   .   .
> Why should not I, a May-game, scorn the weight
> Of my sunk fortunes? snarl at the vices
> Which rot the land, and, without fear or wit,
> Be mine own antic?[56]

---

[51] *ibid.*, IV, iii (Bullen, I, 87).   [52] *ibid.*, I, i (Bullen, I, 11).
[53] *ibid.*, III, ii (Bullen, I, 62).   [54] *ibid.*, II, i (Bullen, I, 31).
[55] *ibid.* (Bullen, I, 28-9).
[56] *ibid.*, I, ii (Bullen, I, 17-18). An independent study of Burton's influence on *The Lovers Melancholy* will be found in G. F. Sensabaugh's "Burton's Influence on Ford's *The Lover's Melancholy*," *Studies in Philology*, XXXIII (1936), 545-71.

THE FANCIES

The principal serious plot of *The Fancies* is a study of mis-understanding: An indigent young lord, Livio, is impatient of slow preferment at the court of the melancholy Octavio, Marquis of Sienna. Being assured by his friend Troylo-Savelli that the marquis is a eunuch, he is persuaded to place his sister Castamela in the "Bower of Fancies," a group of noble maidens who live under the protection of Octavio for his innocent entertainment; and in return he receives from the marquis the office of Master of the Horse. Shortly thereafter Octavio makes advances toward Castamela, which she can only interpret as immoral and insulting, and which she repels. Outraged at her brother's actions, she compliments him with bitter irony upon his advancement and acts the part of a "mistress of the trim." When he is taken in by the act and becomes abusive, she is too deeply insulted by his suspicion to enlighten him.

Meanwhile her melancholy suitor Romanello, who is also ignorant of the true nature of the Bower of Fancies, with Troylo's assistance gains admission to their quarters disguised as a fool, and corroborates his own suspicions. Whereupon, when Livio offers him the hand of Castamela, he scornfully refuses it.

Convinced by these events that his sister is lost to virtue, Livio now quarrels with his friend Troylo-Savelli and demands satisfaction at arms. But before the duel can take place, Octavio makes full explanation: he is the legally appointed guardian, not the lover, of the Fancies; they are daughters of his dead only sister; Troylo drew Castamela into their society so that he might more easily "discover his sincerity" to her; Romanello was allowed to remain in ignorance so that they might examine the nature of his affections. When all doubts are thus satisfied, Troylo is betrothed to Castamela, Octavio nominates a wife from among the Fancies for Livio, and the play ends with a dance in celebration of the betrothals.

The conduct of this play depends upon unjustifiable mystification. Many devious schemes had to be adopted in order to avoid revealing the facts. For example, when Troylo narrates his uncle's tragic history, he enjoins Livio to secrecy at its conclusion. For if the history were known to Livio's family, there would be no misunderstanding between Livio and Casta- mela and therefore none between Livio and Troylo. Again it would be natural for Troylo to enlighten Livio as to his own purpose in enticing Castamela into the Bower, but he does not do so. The reason is again mere dramatic, not logical, necessity. Again, although Troylo drew Castamela into the Bower in order to facilitate his courtship, he does not use the opportunity. For if they came together, Troylo would be obliged to reveal the facts back of his deception, or lose the hand of Castamela. Finally, though Castamela is constantly thrown with the young ladies who are informed of the entire scheme, they carefully conceal it, for no reason, until the next to the last scene in the play. Only with this tissue of improbable concealments is the play kept from falling completely apart.

Octavio, although hardly the central character of the play, contains the clue to its confusing secret: he is melancholy. This time it is a melancholy caused by emasculation—a physical in- jury of a sort not usually discussed, and never, as far as I am aware, accorded sympathetic treatment in the drama previous to Ford. Our great uncle-marquis, explains Troylo-Savelli[1] to the incredulous Livio (II, ii), is impotent—impotent for two emphatic reasons: disabled from birth and rendered more infirm by a deadly wound received in fight against the Turkish galleys. He is never tempted to do more than please his outward senses, whether it be by looking upon fresh beauties, discoursing mer- rily with them, hearing them play and sing, seeing them dance, passing the time with them in pretty amorous questions, riddles, verses of love.[2] All of these are methods of procuring mirth, a principal engine to batter the walls of melancholy, according to Burton. Such pleasure is possible to Octavio, for it is a strange fact that his natural defect does not prevent the flow of a free and full spirit within him;[3] for, as Burton says, nature sees to it that he who has a lame body will be recom-

[1] *The Fancies*, II, ii (Bullen, II, 254).   [2] *ibid.* (Bullen, II, 255).
[3] *ibid.* (Bullen, II, 254).

pensed with an unblemished soul. Octavio's appearance is made
to agree with those famous men of old who were ugly to look
at: he has "a gray beard, wrinkled face, a dried-up marrow,
A toothless head," according to Livio.[4]

Yet, Troylo continues,[5] this bachelor miracle is not free from
the epidemical headache, that is, jealousy; so that he will allow
nobody to be admitted to see the Fancies except members of
his own household; he is suspicious of the musicians who are
permitted to entertain them from time to time, allowing none
to stay longer than an hour, or perhaps two on special days
like this (the wedding-day of Secco and Morosa); finally satis-
fying his qualms about Secco, his barber, by marrying him off
to a jealous guardianess of his virtue, Morosa. Now, according
to Burton, jealousy may be the result of impotency, and especially of the impotency of old men that are cold and dry by
nature, but it is the jealousy such a man has for his *wife* that
is being discussed there. Octavio's is rather one of Burton's
many other jealousies, improperly so called, such as that which
guardians feel toward their wards. So constituted, the old
eunuch has tried to achieve the happiness which fate has denied
him by the absurd conception of his Bower of Fancies. His
surroundings also have been designed so as to palliate as far
as possible the malady under which he labours. Livio catalogues
the charms of the palace and garden at the beginning of the
fateful interview with Troylo. Here they are:

> 'tis a nunnery, a retirement
> For meditation; all the difference extant
> But puzzles only bare belief, not grounds it.
> Rich services in plate, soft and fair lodgings,
> Varieties of recreations, exercise
> Of music in all changes, neat attendance,
> Princely, nay, royal furniture of garments,
> Satiety of gardens, orchards, waterworks,
> Pictures so ravishing that ranging eyes
> Might dwell upon a dotage of conceit
> Without a single wish for livelier substance.[6]

[4] *ibid.*, IV, i (Bullen, II, 289).   [5] *ibid.*, II, ii (Bullen, II, 255-6).
[6] *ibid.* (Bullen, II, 253).

Every last one of these delights we have heard suggested by
Burton under Cure of Melancholy.

In this light on the character of Octavio, his later actions
take on greater consistency than has hitherto been credited to
them. An opportunity having been made for him to see Castamela alone (III, iii), he asks from her only that honourable
affection which he receives from the other Fancies:

> I am not free from passion, though the current
> Of a more lively heat runs slowly through me.[7]

He explains, with an appeal to Platonic doctrine, that love is
but desire of beauty and that it is proper for beauty to desire
to be beloved. But the terms are deceptive, as they would
inevitably be to the seventeenth-century lady accustomed to find
such doctrine the pleasant mask for dishonourable intentions,
and she repulses him with scornful denunciation.

The rebuff spurs Octavio to action. When he next appears
(V, i), the distress of a noisy scandalous quarrel between his
servants Nitido and Secco, and of public misinterpretations of
his honest motives, have been added to the already heavy burden
of an unhappy life. Having grown weary of the whole scheme,
with the inconstancy of the melancholy man, he orders Troylo
to "yield the world account And make clear reckonings."[8] This
is done as soon as the plot to test the seriousness of Romanello's
protestations to Castamela can be concluded to Troylo's satisfaction. A happy ending is huddled up with a masque which
Octavio intends to be "a merriment,"[9] but he himself remains
unhappy. Betrothals and a masque of love only add poignancy
to the fact that love has been forcibly excluded from his experience: the Fancies are his mistresses; indeed he has none other.
The very last words of the play are a fretful rebuke to a society
which will not permit him the harmless invention with which
he has tried to satisfy the yearnings of a damaged body and
spirit: "Great men may be mistook when they mean best."[10]

The mental infection has not been limited to Octavio, but
has spread to another in the play, Romanello. His portraiture

7 *ibid.*, III, iii (Bullen, II, 282).   8 *ibid.*, V, i (Bullen, II, 305).
9 *ibid.*, V, iii (Bullen, II, 320).   10 *ibid.* (Bullen, II, 321).

is sketchy—there is no statement of causes, only a hasty exposition of symptoms, and no cure; but Romanello has another interest all his own. He is the melancholy character in Ford closest in conception to Marston's famous character, the Malcontent, and offers an excellent opportunity to state the relation of Ford's melancholy to malcontentism.

The Malcontent, as illustrated in Malevole, is a double personality: to the people and the court he appears in one light, to his own intimates in an entirely different one. As courtier he is the cynical critic of a hypocritical religion, of an idle, over-fed, wanton society, of a cruel and lying court. He is granted a license similar to that enjoyed by the court fool to speak openly and bawdily, and to insult anybody from court procurer to favourite. He is fantastical and witty.[11] He is marked with many of the characteristics of the animal.[12] In his own true character of Altofronto all this humorous by-play is sloughed off, and a very serious man is revealed underneath. It is exactly as if he removed from himself a disguise which belied not only his appearance, but his words, manner, his very outlook on life. There is still deep hatred of human actions, but it is now of particular men, not of mankind. The present situation of the Court merely puts in brighter relief the old days when

> My throne stood like a point midst of a circle,
> To all of equal nearness; bore with none;
> Rein'd all alike; so slept in fearless virtue,
> Suspectless, too suspectless.[13]

[11] While Sly, one of the actors of the Induction, is insistent that "this play is a bitter play" (Bullen, I, 202), and modern dramatic criticism has agreed, he is also warrant for the belief that the Elizabethan audience found humour as well in Malevole's lines. Burbadge asks Sly why he conceals the feather which was formerly on his hat, and Sly replies, "Why, do you think I'll have jests broken upon me in the play, to be *laughed at?* this play hath beaten all your gallants out of the feathers" (Bullen, I, 201-2). Presumably the audience thought the same of some of the other satirical thrusts, since Sly has "most of the *jests* here in my table-book" (Bullen, I, 200). The Induction, written by Webster and printed in the third quarto of *The Malcontent,* cannot be other than a trustworthy contemporaneous critical document.

[12] For example, his howling, and appetite as "unsatiable as the grave," *The Malcontent,* I, i (Bullen, I, 210-11).

[13] *The Malcontent,* I, i (Bullen, I, 219).

His manner of insolence is replaced by sober and affectionate regard toward his only faithful friend Celso. The vulgar jests and bestial noises are gone completely, and remembered with loathing.[14] In a word, he admits that as Malevole the Malcontent he "plays discontented," just as a child would say he "plays mad." The character is a pose, a disguise worn for self-protection,[15] while he observes the march of events and advances his own cause. What then is the true man, minus the mask? More than anything else the shocked, disillusioned man, terribly intent—so intent that he cannot sleep and is haunted by dreams "the most fantastical"[16]—upon bringing to justice certain individuals who have done wrong. He is discontented, yes, but far from helpless like the melancholic: he is a man of action, a plot-master, planning and expecting success in his devices:

> *Mal.*   Hope, hope, that ne'er forsak'st the wretched'st man,
> Yet bidd'st me live, and lurk in this disguise!
> What, play I well the free-breath'd discontent?
> Why, man, we are all philosophical monarchs
> Or natural fools. Celso, the court's a-fire;
> The duchess' sheets will smoke for't ere't be long:
> Impure Mendoza, that sharp-nos'd lord, that made
> The cursèd match link'd Genoa with Florence,
> Now broad-horns the duke, which he now knows.
> Discord to malcontents is very manna:
> When the ranks are burst, then scuffle, Altofront.
> *Celso*   Ay, but durst——
> *Mal.*   'Tis gone; 'tis swallow'd like a mineral:
> Some way 'twill work; pheut, I'll not shrink:
> He's resolute who can no lower sink.[17]

---

[14] *ibid.*, V, ii (Bullen, I, 301) : "O God, how loathsome this toying is to me!"
[15] *ibid.*, I, i (Bullen, I, 219) :
       "What, play I well the free-breath'd discontent?"
   III, i (Bullen, I, 264) :
       "O, my disguise fools him most powerfully!
       For that I seem a desperate malcontent;"
   V, ii (Bullen, I, 301) :
       "Better play the fool lord than be the fool lord."
[16] *ibid.*, I, i (Bullen, I, 213).
[17] *ibid.* (Bullen, I, 219-20).

The traditional malcontent owes something to earlier trea-
tises on melancholy, as Stoll[18] and Walley[19] have pointed out.
Of Romanello, however, Ford made a much more Burtonian
figure than a mere malcontent. The dual nature of Malevole
is resolved: Romanello has a single, not a dual personality.
His discontent has become· "an habit, *morbus sonticus, or
chronicus*, a chronick or continute disease," instead of a disguise which can be worn at will. He can hardly wait to be
refused in his suit to Castamela before he bursts forth with
direct personal insult like Malevole:

> A dog, a parrot,
> A monkey, a caroch, a guarded lackey,
> A waiting-woman with her lips seal'd up,
> Are pretty toys to please my Mistress Wanton![20]

Like Malevole he condemns all society in his abuse of the
female sex:

> all women
> Would prostitute all honour to the luxury
> Of ease and titles.[21]

Like Malevole he has certain affinities with the animal: he
concludes he will

> converse with beasts; there is in mankind
> No sound society,[22]

though he does not imitate the beast as Malevole does when
he howls. It should be noted, however, that Malevole, the man
with the disguise, can talk so and be laughed at: Romanello,
with only one self, can only be interpreted as deadly serious.
His insults are accordingly beyond forgiveness and beyond
explanation, unless he be charitably called mad (or melancholic)
in his own proper person. So Castamela takes him: " 'tis a madness I have not oft observ'd";[23] so also his sister Flavia: "poor
gentleman, He bears a troubled mind."[24] And as soon as Casta-

---

[18] "Shakspere, Marston, and the Malcontent Type," *Modern Philology*,
III, 281-303.

[19] *The Malcontent.*

[20] *The Fancies*, I, iii (Bullen, II, 239).

[21] *ibid.*

[22] *ibid.*, IV, ii (Bullen, II, 295).

[23] *ibid.*, I, iii (Bullen, II, 239).

[24] *ibid.*, III, ii (Bullen, II, 274).

mela is taken off to join the Fancies, he is determined "to pursue
the trick on't,"[25] not with any logical and remedial plan such as
Altofronto-Malevole's, but only an unhappy desire to corroborate his worst fears.

Like Malevole he assumes a disguise (as Signor Prugnuolo)
in order that he may

> study,
> Amongst the ladies, in a formal foppery,
> To vent some curiosity of language
> Above their apprehensions,   .   .   .
>
> .   .   .   .   .   .
> Now amorous, then scurvy, sometimes bawdy.[26]

But Romanello is not "playing discontented": he talks in this
vein always, even to his love (I, iii), his sister, and his friend
(IV, ii). His disguise is a change in appearance only, not a
change in words, manner, or outlook; and even that fools
nobody.[27] Besides, in the disguise scene he does not say anything really witty, as Malevole does, but rather gives tart
answers to problems of love, all of which are drawn, suitably
enough, from The Anatomy: that love upsets a man's standards
of judgment ("renders a wise man fool, and a fool wise");[28]
that therefore the lover thinks his mistress beautiful even if
she be "the old, the fool, the ugly and deform'd";[29] that love
produces antithetical emotions ("pleasure, travail; bitter, sweet;
war, peace");[30] that love ends in despair and violent death;[31]
that women in love are more jealous than men.[32]

To conclude, all that is particularly morose of character and
insulting of utterance in Malevole is retained in Romanello; all
that is hopeful, constructive, and amusing in Malevole is rejected. Romanello, though presented in only a few hasty pictures, is Malevole rewritten into a complete melancholic and
a fit complementary piece to the main melancholy character of
the play.

[25] ibid., I, iii (Bullen, II, 245).
[27] ibid., V, iii (Bullen, II, 320).
[29] ibid. (Bullen, II, 278).
[31] ibid.

[26] ibid., III, i (Bullen, II, 266).
[28] ibid., III, iii (Bullen, II, 277).
[30] ibid. (Bullen, II, 277).
[32] ibid. (Bullen, II, 279).

THE BROKEN HEART

The Broken Heart is a tale of many broken hearts. Ithocles, the inordinately ambitious young favourite and military general of aged King Amyclas of Sparta, has forced his sister Penthea to marry Bassanes, a rich old man. This politic marriage proves a torment of jealousy to him and an agony of grief to her, since she is still in love with young Orgilus, son of Crotolon, Counsellor of State, to whom she was originally betrothed. Orgilus, believing that he can lighten Bassanes's fear and Penthea's sadness by going away, announces that he is journeying to Athens. Actually, in disguise as a student, he enters the "oratory" of the philosopher Tecnicus in hopes of finding a balm for his own disappointed love. When it chances one day that Penthea walks alone in the palace grove near the oratory, and Orgilus comes upon her, his resolve breaks down and he renews his old suit; she resists him with pity but determination. Convinced, then, that he can balance the scales of justice only by the murder of Ithocles, Orgilus throws off his disguise and returns to court. Ithocles, now repenting the suffering he has caused, greets his return with a new friendliness, which facilitates Orgilus's plans for revenge.

The royal princess Calantha and Ithocles, meanwhile, have fallen in love, and Amyclas consents to their betrothal even though a suitor of more nearly equal station, Nearchus, Prince of Argos, has come at this time to arrange his marriage with the princess. And Bassanes, too, is repentant and is trying to reform, but too late. When Penthea, tortured by his jealous brutalities, goes mad and dies of a broken heart, Orgilus avenges her tragedy by the murder of Ithocles. At a court dance intended to celebrate the marriage of Prophilus (Ithocles's friend) and Euphranea (Orgilus's sister), messengers bring in turn the news of the death of the king, of Penthea, of Ithocles. Calantha is stricken to the heart, but sees the dance ceremoniously through to the end. She then condemns Orgilus to death, nominates Nearchus her successor as sovereign of Sparta, marries the corpse of Ithocles, and herself dies of a broken heart.

Bassanes is the chief melancholic of *The Broken Heart*.
Orgilus describes his affliction at the outset of the play (I, i) :

> *Org.*   Bassanes,
> The man that calls her wife, considers truly
> What heaven of perfection he is lord of
> By thinking faire Penthea his: this thought
> Begets a kinde of monster-love, which love
> Is nurse unto a feare so strong and servile
> As brands all dotage with a jealousie.
> All eyes who gaze upon that shrine of beauty
> He doth resolve doe homage to the miracle;
> Some one, he is assur'd, may now or then,
> If opportunity but sort, prevaile:
> So much out of a selfe-unworthinesse
> His feares transport him; not that he findes cause
> In her obedience, but his owne distrust.
> *Crot.*   You spin out your discourse.
> *Org.*   My griefs are violente:
> For knowing how the maid was heretofore
> Courted by me, his jealousies grow wild
> That I should steale again into her favours,
> And undermine her vertues; which the gods
> Know I nor dare nor dreame of.[1]

All the essentials are here: Bassanes finds himself lord of a
beautiful woman; the thought pleases him but engenders in
him the post-marital disorder, jealousy; it is characterized
chiefly by such fear that he cannot avoid suspecting everybody;
and that without cause, for her obedience is spotless; it is Bassanes's distrust, directed especially against Orgilus himself, that
is making for Penthea "a most barbarous thraldome, misery,
Affliction"[2] of her life on earth. Elsewhere—indeed wherever
Orgilus appears in the play—he keeps up a running commen-
tary on Bassanes's affliction. To all the others in the court
Bassanes is proverbial; for example Grausis thinks "You dote,
You are beside yourselfe";[3] Prophilus: "Hee's distracted";[4]
Hemophil: "most admirable lunacy";[5] Ithocles: "His jealousie

---

[1] *The Broken Heart*, I, i (Sherman, pp. 142-3).
[2] *ibid.* (Sherman, p. 141).   [3] *ibid.*, II, i (Sherman, p. 171).
[4] *ibid.*, III, ii (Sherman, p. 197).   [5] *ibid.* (Sherman, p. 198).

has rob'd him of his wits; 'A talkes 'a knowes not what";[6] and even Bassanes himself acknowledges "a desperate wound," a "breach of reason."[7]

Bassanes's first appearance occurs in Act II, Scene i, a scene laid in his house and given almost entirely into his hands. The two chief characteristics of jealousy, as made clear in the definition, are strongly set forth in the scene as a whole: 1) he is consumed with fear that Penthea will prove unfaithful to him, and sets two ignoble servants, Phulas and Grausis to watch over her. On this subject he is a veritable *ars amatoria*, culled from the parts of *The Anatomy* dealing with Love-Melancholy and Jealousy: "There's a lust Committed by the eye, that sweats and travels, Plots, wakes, contrives"[8] till the deed is consummated. Therefore, echoing Volpone,[9] he'll "have that window next the street dam'd up; It gives too full a prospect to temptation, And courts a gazers glances." The smallest written note is not to be conveyed to Penthea, for "it may prove A mysticall preparative to lewdnesse."[10] All women are false, there exists not one "but can fall, and doth, or would,"[11] and the beautiful are always immoral,[12] whether she be a city housewife stroking the head which she has branched, a dame at court raising her husband up on stilts of office by means of her own shame, or a country girl hiding her trespass under blushes of assumed innocence. 2) He is equally afraid that he will not be able to hold the affection of his wife. For this reason he tries pathetically to please her by every means within his power and wealth: she will go to court to meet her brother in such array that every lady will fret with envy; they will leave this melancholy house and move to a "delightfull island"; she will choose what recreations, what company she pleases; if only she will chase the sadness from her brow:

> For my sake put on a more chearefull mirth;
> Thou't marre thy cheekes, and make me old in griefes.[13]

[6] *ibid.*
[7] *ibid.* (Sherman, p. 199).
[8] *ibid.*, II, i (Sherman, p. 163).
[9] *ibid.* (Pointed out by Sherman, p. 273).
[10] *ibid.* (Sherman, p. 164).
[11] *ibid.* (Sherman, p. 165).
[12] *ibid.* (Sherman, p. 166): "Why to be faire Should yeeld presumption of a faulty soule?"
[13] *ibid.* (Sherman, p. 169).

And it is because old Grausis presumes to speak to Penthea
with less than courtly consideration that she receives Bassanes's
bitterest scourging "leave chattering, mag-pye," "furies whip
thee!" "jugling bawd," "I'le have you pounded," "damnable
bitch-foxe!" "I'le spit thee on a stake, Or chop thee into
collops!"[14] That Bassanes is finding jealousy what Burton calls
"a most intolerable burden, a madness itself" is clear both from
the anguish he expresses[15] in asides, and from the emotions
which Ford has objectified more or less subtly in the sweat
which streams from his face as Grausis recalls that he is
childless:

> What thinke'ee,
> If your fresh lady breed young bones, my lord?
> Wood not a chopping boy d'ee good at heart?[16]

Practically all of the circumstances that Burton pointed out
as likely to induce jealousy, are also indicated in this scene:
Sparta has a hot climate; Bassanes is a scambling old man,[17]
about whom there is more than a suggestion of the impotency
of old age;[18] his ugliness is strongly contrasted with the unusual
beauty of Penthea; and Penthea is as yet childless.[19] These facts

---

[14] ibid. (Sherman, p. 167-9).

[15] ibid. (Sherman, pp. 166, 170, 171):
> "Swormes of confusion huddle in my thoughts
> In rare distemper."
> "A tympany swels in my head already."
> "My agonies are infinite."

[16] ibid. (Sherman, p. 169).

[17] ibid., IV, ii (Sherman, p. 231):
> "Wisdome, looke'ee, begins
> To rave!—art thou mad too, antiquity?"

[18] ibid., II, i (Sherman, p. 167):
> "Grausis   What, lady! laugh,
> Be merry; time is precious."

[19] Miss Cochnower, Seventeenth Century Studies, p. 153, n. 37, points to the
following evidence that Bassanes is barren: 1) "Grausis . . . twits him with
the possibility of Penthea producing 'a chopping boy.'" [The Broken Heart,
II, i, Sherman, p. 169]. 2) "Orgilus calls him 'thou barren rocke.'" [ibid., IV,
ii, Sherman, p. 229]. 3) "Penthea, in her madness, complains of her childless-
ness, concluding, ''tis not my fault.'" [ibid., Sherman, p. 231]. 4) "Bassanes
himself, addressing Penthea, says: 'O that I could preserve thee in fruition
As in devotion!'" [ibid., III, ii, Sherman, p. 199].

make all the more pointed Grausis's sneer about breeding young bones.

Thus far Bassanes has been shown to us only in the security of his own home. In later scenes, when he has, through his great love for Penthea, submitted her to the dangers and temptations of life at court, even more barbarous symptoms come to the fore. In Act II, Scene ii, the conversation turns to the marriage of Euphranea and Prophilus; Bassanes re-phrases *The Anatomy* to describe the blessedness of the marriage state:

> The joyes of marriage are the heaven on earth,
> Life's paradise, great princesse, the soules quiet,
> Sinewes of concord, earthly immortality,
> Eternity of pleasures; no restoratives
> Like to a constant woman![20]

He says what he sincerely believes, but his remarks only lend contrast to his repugnant suspicions about the unhappy woman who shares with him this "blessed" state. An appointment between Ithocles and his sister gives rise to the darkest of all the fears which harass the jealous man—incest. Act III, Scene ii, shows him acting on this suspicion, first eavesdropping in Ithocles's bedchamber where he has no right to be, then, fulfilling the prognostics by threatening to murder brother and sister in revenge for their supposed crime. Ford could not have chosen a more dramatic moment than this to show his character undergoing one of the sudden changes symptomatic of jealousy. Bassanes has been demanding blood, has been making the strange eyes and gestures of the melancholic,[21] but his rage quiets at the "sounds caelestiall"[22] of Penthea's voice, and in a moment he is on his knees, begging her to say that he has never given her one ill word!

When at the end of Act III, Scene ii, Ithocles takes Penthea into his care because he dare not trust her any longer to the

[20] *The Broken Heart*, II, ii (Sherman, p. 176).
[21] *ibid.*, III, ii (Sherman, p. 198):
> "How 'a stares,
> Struts, puffes, and sweats: most admirable lunacy!"
[22] *ibid.* (Sherman, p. 200).

jealous husband's fury, Bassanes reaches the breaking point. "Diseases desperate must find cures alike," he says,[23] darkly foreshadowing madness, injury, murder, or despair—the usual prognostics of incurable jealousy. Before the opening of Act IV, Scene ii, however, he has found his refuge: patience—the only final and sure cure of jealousy. Hereafter he is a changed man, yet a perfectly consistent type, except to the spectator who might be unfamiliar with the treatise that Ford is illustrating. "Henceforth I'le study reformation,"[24] Bassanes says. He leaves off his brutal treatment of the servants[25] and gives them "liberty at home, abroad, at all times." At this Phulas mutters, recurring to Grausis's old jibe about impotency, that the change in Bassanes's temper must be due to his having been gelded—one of Burton's methods of driving out one nail with another. Bassanes declares his sorrow at having been verier beast than a beast in doubting his wife, determining to put before the incensed deities "a largesse of more patience Then their displeased altars can require."[26] Patience characterizes him in the way he endures the distressing frenzies of Penthea (IV, ii), and the sorrow at the public announcement of the three deaths (where he compares himself with pride to Calantha who did not pule like a girl with a finger in her eye) (V, ii). Indeed he does not wholly give way to his grief until the last moment of the play (V, iii) where he does so for a characteristically ironic reason: Calantha, who suffered so much so sadly in life, smiles in death. Bassanes thus remains consistent to his Burtonian type to the very end, and is only wholly cured of his jealousy by that event (the death of Penthea) which is inescapably conclusive to his part.

Ithocles is the Burtonian character next in importance. He is first seen in a most favourable light (I, ii). Returning home from a successful military campaign which has brought Messene under the domination of Sparta, he is received with tremendous acclaim. Amyclas, the old king, feels his heart leap with new vigour and wants to build a temple in honour of the conquering

[23] *ibid.* (Sherman, p. 201).   [24] *ibid.*, IV, ii (Sherman, p. 227).
[25] See especially Act II, Scene i; Act II, Scene iii.
[26] *The Broken Heart*, IV, ii (Sherman, p. 228).

hero. Prophilus, who was present at the battle, praises Ithocles's extreme modesty: "He hath serv'd his country, And thinks 'twas but his duty."[27] Armostes is proud to claim him as a blood relative. The Princess Calantha weaves a chaplet with her own hands and crowns his head. Ithocles receives all this with the blushing modesty Prophilus noted, and, in the best tradition of the officer, tries to pass the credit on to his men.

But it is necessary, even more than is usually the case in Ford, to know Ithocles's past history. Orgilus, who introduced Bassanes, supplies this information. Ithocles was once powerless and discontented. He then chanced to become the favourite of the old king, and, proud at being so distinguished while yet so young, set out to confirm himself in wealth and power. He forced his sister to marry Bassanes, a nobleman high in honour and riches, and treated the impecunious rejected suitor, Orgilus, with arrogance and scorn.[28] Orgilus never relaxes his resentment for this treatment, even though he admits, after murdering Ithocles, that there never lived a gentleman of greater merit, promise, or "abiliment to steere a kingdome"[29] than Ithocles. Only so far can Orgilus go. Ithocles himself is needed to explain that his actions were motivated by ambition, which has now begun to take its toll in "sicknesse" of the mind. He has tried to assuage his melancholy by taking counsel with his friends (as Burton suggested), but finds that nothing short of medication or removal of the cause—and that quickly—will effect his cure:

> Ambition! 'tis of vipers breed; it knawes
> A passage through the wombe that gives it motion.
> .   .   .   .   Morality
> .   physicks not the sicknesse of a minde
> Broken with griefes: strong feavers are not eas'd
> With counsell, but with best receipts and meanes:
> Meanes, speedy meanes and certaine; that's the cure.[30]

He is sorry now for what his ambition and the heat of unsteady youth, green indiscretion, wilfulness, and deceptive flattery led

[27] *ibid.*, I, ii (Sherman, p. 147).
[28] *ibid.*, I, i (Sherman, p. 141) and III, iv (Sherman, p. 207).
[29] *ibid.*, V, ii (Sherman, p. 257).   [30] *ibid.*, II, ii (Sherman, pp. 171-2).

him to do,[31] and abjectly apologizes to Penthea for his cruelty.[32]
He tries even to make it up to Orgilus (III, iii), who, in his
truculence, takes it in the worst sense:

> lordly Ithocles
> Hath grac'd my entertainment in abundance;
> Too humbly hath descended from that height
> Of arrogance and spleene which wrought the rape
> On griev'd Penthea's purity: his scorne
> Of my untoward fortunes is reclaim'd
> Unto a courtship, almost to a fawning.[33]

Ithocles is melancholy as a result of an excess of the passion
of ambition. Those around him begin to notice, as always in
Ford, the signs of his affliction: Prophilus, his best friend, notes
that "sadnesse growes Upon his recreations"[34] and Bassanes
reports his being taken with an unaccountable fit, so serious that
fear is expressed for his life.[35]

Although Ithocles is sorry for the results of his ambition, it
still impells him strongly in other directions. He has now set
his heart upon marriage with the loftiest lady in the kingdom,
Princess Calantha, and he dares to insult his rival, Nearchus,
a foreign prince (IV, i). In his insolent behaviour with Nearchus, we see the arrogantly ambitious Ithocles whom Orgilus
talks about. Armostes undertakes to warn Ithocles of the purely
politic dangers of ambition:

> Containe your selfe, my lord: Ixion, ayming
> To embrace Juno, bosom'd but a cloud,
> And begat Centaures: 'tis an useful morall;[36]

as well as upon its dangers to mental health:

> Quiet
> These vaine unruly passions, which will render ye
> Into a madnesse.[37]

Ithocles attains his goal, he is betrothed to Calantha (IV, iii),
but meets the revenger before the marriage can be performed.

[31] ibid. (Sherman, pp. 173-4).   [32] ibid., III, ii (Sherman, p. 193).
[33] ibid., III, iv (Sherman, p. 207).   [34] ibid., II, iii (Sherman, p. 179).
[35] ibid. (Sherman, p. 186).   [36] ibid., IV, i (Sherman, pp. 221-2).
[37] ibid. (Sherman, p. 224).

Ambition remains the keynote of his character to the very end:
Orgilus taunts him with it as he prepares to kill him:

> You dream't of kingdomes, did 'ee? how to bosome
> The delicacies of a youngling princesse;
> How with this nod to grace that subtill courtier,
> How with that frowne to make this noble tremble,
> And so forth.[38]

And Ithocles in his last words bids farewell to ambition, along
with beauty, youth and love.[39] His violent death is the one
Burton prophesied for the ambitious man.

While Burtonian melancholy does not extend over the state
of Sparta as it did over Cyprus in *The Lovers Melancholy*, it
does bring disaster to the ruling dynasty and to two noble
families. And two other characters are affected. One is Penthea.
Her distressed husband (who indeed should have been skillful)
observes the fearful signs of melancholy: that Penthea has been
ill he twice reports[40] to members of the court; her sadness is
evidently construed as abnormal—Grausis believes her charge
to be "over-sad,"[41] and Bassanes tries to relieve it by extreme
means (bribes, entreaties) now that more ordinary means have
failed. At last resort he suggests a "change of air"—that they
move away from their present residence which "stands . . .
too much inward" and "is too melancholy."[42] Penthea herself,
especially after Orgilus[43] has put in her mind the seed of the
idea that she is living in whoredom with Bassanes, is conscious
of the fact that her sorrows have taken root, so to speak, and
becomes uncontrollable. On two occasions she makes clear statement of this belief, once to Ithocles, agreeing generously to help
his suit with Calantha:

> If sorrowes
> Have not too much dull'd my *infected* braine,
> I'le cheere invention for an active straine;[44]

[38] *ibid.*, IV, iv (Sherman, p. 248).   [39] *ibid.* (Sherman, p. 250).
[40] *ibid.*, II, i (Sherman, p. 170); II, ii (Sherman, p. 175).
[41] *ibid.*, II, i (Sherman, p. 166).   [42] *ibid.* (Sherman, p. 168).
[43] *ibid.*, II, iii (Sherman, pp. 182, 183).
[44] *ibid.*, III, ii (Sherman, p. 197). Italics mine.

once to Calantha in the witty device (the legacy) by which she carries out that promise:

> beauty, pompe,
> With every sensuality our giddinesse
> Doth frame an idoll, are unconstant friends
> When any *troubled passion* makes assault
> On the unguarded castle of the mind.[45]

In the end, as we know, she goes mad, and satisfies the most calamitous prognostication of the authorities in taking her own life in a way only too familiar to them, by refusing to sleep, eat, or drink.[46]

And, finally, Orgilus, the other lover of *The Broken Heart*, is troubled with the dread malady of Bassanes and Ithocles and Penthea. For the most part he is drawn along the conventional lines of the pastoral lover: absence from Penthea will be banishment to him;[47] he has grown thin and pale with the pangs of love; he looks like the ruins of the ruins of his youth.[48] He knows, however, in addition something of an unaccountable and uncontrollable mental distress. He says prophetically as he leaves on his supposed travels that a change of air will do him no good,[49] and acknowledges an "unsetled minde"[50] to his lecturer Tecnicus. Tecnicus observes in his looks an increasing and dangerous tension.[51] His father recognizes melancholy full grown when he fears

> Thou hast brought backe a worse infection with thee,
> Infection of thy mind; which, as thou sayst,
> Threatens the desolation of our family.[52]

[45] *ibid.*, III, v (Sherman, p. 212). Italics mine.
[46] *ibid.*, IV, ii (Sherman, pp. 233-4):
> "*Itho.* Christalla, Philema, when slept my sister,
> Her ravings are so wild?
> *Christalla*   Sir, not these ten dayes.
> *Philema* We watch by her continually; besides,
> We cannot any way pray her to eat."

[47] *ibid.*, II, iii (Sherman, p. 181).   [48] *ibid.* (Sherman, p. 185).
[49] *ibid.*, I, i (Sherman, p. 145).   [50] *ibid.*, I, iii (Sherman, p. 154).
[51] *ibid.*, III, i (Sherman, p. 188).   [52] *ibid.*, III, iv (Sherman, p. 208).

LOVES SACRIFICE

The principal plot of *Loves Sacrifice* deals with a jealous husband and his revenge. The melancholy old Philippo Caraffa, Duke of Pavy, has married a beautiful lady, Bianca, in spite of her low station and his senate's express wish that he marry a princess. Fernando, the duke's young favourite, falls in love with the duchess and lays repeated siege to her virtue. Bianca resists him four times, but at length, grown weary of her distasteful marriage bargain, comes to his bedroom and offers herself to him freely but with the assertion that she will kill herself if he accepts. He declines this sacrifice.

Meanwhile the duke's sister Fiormonda, recently a widow, has set her cap for Fernando. Enraged when he rejects her, and already suspicious of Bianca, she vengefully sets her agent D'Avolos to spy on the lovers and then to feed the duke's mind with suspicion. Though naturally disposed to jealousy Philippo gives Bianca a chance to defend herself, but is no longer able to resist Fiormonda and D'Avolos when their accusations become direct. At length D'Avolos leads Philippo into a chamber where he can see his wife and Fernando, who believe the duke to be bathing for his health in the springs at Lucca, in each other's arms. Philippo breaks in upon them and murders Bianca. Fernando refuses to fight, once Bianca is dead, and thus convinces the duke that his duchess was "chaste." At Bianca's ceremonious funeral Fernando kills himself with poison and Philippo stabs himself. The dukedom reverting to Fiormonda, she bestows it upon an old suitor named Roseilli by taking his hand in marriage. Roseilli accepts it and at once condemns D'Avolos to death by starvation and forswears Fiormonda's bed forever.

Duke Philippo Caraffa is the melancholic in *Loves Sacrifice*. He suffers from two melancholies in succession, which I shall ask the reader to distinguish one from the other under the names of plain "melancholy" and "jealous melancholy" in the following analysis. Petruchio's initial description of Philippo's

melancholy has unfortunately dropped out in the printing, except
for a few lines, tantalizing in their incompleteness :

> Now, nephew, as I told you, since the duke
> Hath held the reins of state in his own hand,
> Much alter'd from the man he was before,—
>
> .   .   .   .   .   .
>
> As if he were transformèd in his mind,—
> To soothe him in his pleasures, amongst whom
> Is fond Ferentes; one whose pride takes pride
> In nothing more than to delight his lust.[1]

Although this is fragmentary, we can still observe Philippo's
peculiarities in his actions. He suffers the causeless sorrow of
the melancholy man, pausing in the midst of the antics of
Roseilli, the fool, to envy Roseilli's happiness[2] as contrasted
with his unhappiness. He struggles constantly to be rid of this
sorrow by doing things which will distract his mind: hunting,[3]
riding or watching riding,[4] for these exercises are cures of
melancholy. Or he entertains himself with ridiculous perform-
ances, whether they be regularly planned, as is Ferentes's ill-
starred masque before the Abbot of Monaco,[5] or by accident,
as at the rehearsal of Mauruccio's courtship (II, i), or the
clowning of Roseilli (III, ii) ; for mirth is a remedy. Philippo
hopes "we have found A salve for melancholy,—mirth and
ease."[6] In fact he is ready to follow the lead of any trifler who
can "soothe him in his pleasures,"[7] even if he be one like
Ferentes who delights only in lust. He is strongly marked with
the melancholy man's inconstancy: he incessantly desires a new
form of amusement, taking eagerly to the clowning of Mauruccio, Roseilli, and Giacopo (III, ii), after having rejected a

---

[1] *Loves Sacrifice*, I, i (Bullen, II, 11-12). This is probably the largest
lacuna in the text of Ford as we have it. Others occur in *Loves Sacrifice*, V,
i (Bullen, II, 89) and in *The Broken Heart*, II, iii (Sherman, p. 180). On the
last named, see Bradbrook, *Themes and Conventions*, p. 260.

[2] *Loves Sacrifice*, III, ii (Bullen, II, 64-5).

[3] *ibid.*, I, i (Bullen, II, 12) ; II, ii (Bullen, II, 40).

[4] *ibid.*, I, ii (Bullen, II, 27).

[5] *ibid.*, III, iv. The performance which takes place here was ordered in Act
III, Scene ii (Bullen, II, 60-1).

[6] *ibid.*, II, i (Bullen, II, 33).

[7] *ibid.*, I, i (Bullen, II, 12).

suggestion that they play maw, with "The game's too tedious";[8]
he is always seeking new surroundings and new waters[9]—at
once a symptom of his disease and an attempt to cure it. He
is equally changeable in disposition: sputtering in anger at
Roseilli's uncommissioned visit to the Spanish court just a
moment after he has been loudly laughing with Ferentes about
Mauruccio.[10] Such is the picture of the man which is presented
to us before Act III, Scene ii, where there is an important
development.

Philippo's melancholy is, then, the most unexplainable of all
other major cases in Ford, as far as its cause is concerned.
Philippo's quick anger at Roseilli and his own realization that
he is choleric,[11] together with his physical indisposition and
headache[12] and his alacrity in meeting death[13] may mean that
his is a simple physical maladjustment—distemperature caused
by an adustion of the humour choler. Slow at first to anger at
Fernando and Bianca, when once he satisfies his mind that
Bianca has sinned, he gives free rein to his choler and is forever referring to it.[14] Or again there are several indications
that his is a melancholy resulting from ambition and self-love:
the fact that he is "much alter'd from the man he was" since
he "hath held the reins of state in his own hand";[15] the fact
that he is given to emphasizing the dignity of courts and the
respect due to himself from courtiers.[16] It is not likely that
perfect assurance in the matter of cause can be reached with the
text as it stands. At all events Ford makes Philippo a definitely
melancholy man, and no more is necessary for the course his
character is to follow in the rest of the play.

[8] *ibid.*, III, ii (Bullen, II, 63).   [9] *ibid.*, IV, ii (Bullen, II, 85-6).
[10] *ibid.*, I, ii (Bullen, II, 26-8).
[11] *ibid.* (Bullen, II, 28):
           "Let's strive to overpass this choleric heat."
[12] *ibid.*, III, ii (Bullen, II, 62):   "I feel
                 As 'twere a disposition to be sick;
                 My head is ever aching."
[13] *ibid.*, V, iii (Bullen, II, 106).
[14] *ibid.*, IV, i (Bullen, II, 75); V, i (Bullen, II, 90, 92); V, ii (Bullen,
II, 100); V, iii (Bullen, II, 103).
[15] *ibid.*, I, i (Bullen, II, 11).
[16] *ibid.* (Bullen, II, 14); III, ii (Bullen, II, 62).

This plain melancholy is the first of four causes of Philippo's jealous melancholy and of the tragedy which overtakes him. "Melancholy men are apt to be jealous, and jealous apt to be melancholy," Burton explains. The mental distraction being already fully developed, Philippo falls a ready victim to (the second cause) D'Avolos's well-plotted insinuations against Bianca's chastity. These are presented exactly in the manner of Iago moulding the opinion of Othello: in the first scene[17] muttering inexplicit but harassing accusations to the husband in the presence of the accused wife, and then refusing to explain them; in the second scene[18] speaking aloud and more explicitly to the husband alone; and so by successive steps in the following scenes leading him up to passionate disappointment, rage, and murder.

The third cause of Philippo's jealous melancholy is his ugliness and lack of grace, a good ground, Burton says. Bianca damns him to his face with crooked legs, scambling feet, a tolerable face, wearish hands, bloodless lips, and an untrimmed beard.

> I wonder you could think 'twere possible,
> When I had once but look'd on your Fernando,
> I ever could love you again.[19]

The fourth and most important cause of Philippo's jealous melancholy is a dramatization of the failure to observe another of Burton's provisions: that husband and wife should be equal in years, birth, fortune, virtue, education—in fact in everything if possible. This theme is so constantly reiterated that one concludes it is one of the central thoughts of the play. Bianca is not the equal of Philippo in birth, fortune, or virtue. Even before there was a shadow of jealousy in Philippo's mind, he reveals consciousness of weakness in his position by defending his marriage:

> Though my gray-headed senate in the laws
> Of strict opinion and severe dispute
> Would tie the limits of our free affects,—

[17] Othello, III, iii; Loves Sacrifice, III, ii.
[18] Othello, IV, i; Loves Sacrifice, III, iii.
[19] Loves Sacrifice, V, i (Bullen, II, 92).

Like superstitious Jews,—to match with none
But in a tribe of princes like ourselves,
Gross-nurtur'd slaves, who force their wretched souls
To crouch to profit; nay, for trash and wealth
Dote on some crookèd or misshapen form;
Hugging wise nature's lame deformity,
Begetting creatures ugly as themselves:—
But why should princes do so, that command
The storehouse of the earth's hid minerals?—
No, my Bianca, thou'rt to me as dear
As if thy portion had been Europe's riches.[20]

What is Bianca's station? She is in one place "daughter Unto
a gentleman of Milán—no better—Preferr'd to serve i' th'
Duke of Milan's court,"[21] and in her own words, "a simple
gentlewoman."[22] The discovery of her supposed amour with
Fernando loosens the tongues of Fiormonda and Philippo in
a way exaggerated by the passion of the moment, but fairly
conveying Philippo's and the court's estimation of Bianca's very
great inferiority. The Duke believes

It should not be:—Bianca! why, I took her
From lower than a bondage.[23]

Fiormonda says the same things more openly—that Bianca was
headed toward something distinct from marriage with a prince:

What is she but the sallow-colour'd brat
Of some unlanded bankrupt, taught to catch
The easy fancies of young prodigal bloods
In springes of her stew-instructed art?—
Here's your most virtuous duchess![24]

The sharp-witted Fiormonda notes three of the four causes
—an already melancholy mind, victimization by D'Avolos,
Bianca's difference in birth and conditions—in conversation
with Fernando. Her analysis of Philippo's jealous melancholy

[20] *ibid.*, I, i (Bullen, II, 15-16).   [21] *ibid.* (Bullen, II, 12).
[22] *ibid.*, V, i (Bullen, II, 93).   [23] *ibid.*, III, iii (Bullen, II, 69).
[24] *ibid.*, IV, i (Bullen, II, 74).

is a companion piece to Petruchio's (fragmentary) analysis of
his plain melancholy.

> *Fior.*   What would you say, my lord,
> If he, out of some melancholy spleen,
> Edg'd-on by some thank-picking parasite,
> Should now prove jealous? I mistrust it shrewdly.
> *Fern.*   What, madam! jealous?
> *Fior.*   Yes; for but observe,
> A prince whose eye is chooser to his heart
> Is seldom steady in the lists of love,
> Unless the party he affects do match
> His rank in equal portion or in friends:
> I never yet, out of report, or else
> By warranted description, have observ'd
> The nature of fantastic jealousy,
> If not in him.[25]

"By warranted description" comes close to a direct reference to
Burton. Like Corax and Orgilus and Muretto, she has given
The Anatomy not only reading but close study. Others in the
court as well have noticed his jealous melancholy: Petruchio
finds him "lately much distemper'd"[26] and Nibrassa, "a jealous
madman."[27]

From the first scene of the fourth act the die of Philippo's
actions is cast, and he ceases to be noticeably individualized.
Like Bassanes he goes through the jealous man's changeable-
ness: successive feelings of outrage and pitying sorrow, threatening to cut Bianca's flesh to shreds at one moment and then
begging that she forgive him, that he is mad, at another.[28] He
soon develops the violence of the jealous man, and fulfils the
direst but most expected prognostication of this most violent
form of melancholy by murdering his wife and causing the
death of his friend.

'TIS PITTY

The chief plot of *'Tis Pitty* is a story of incest between
brother and sister. Giovanni, the brilliantly educated son of a

25 *ibid.* (Bullen, II, 81-2).   26 *ibid.*, IV, ii (Bullen, II, 86).
27 *ibid.*, V, ii (Bullen, II, 97).   28 *ibid.*, IV, ii (Bullen, II, 85).

Parman citizen, Florio, falls in love with his sister Annabella. Wishing to justify himself in philosophy and religion, he confesses to his spiritual advisor, Friar Bonaventura, who warns him against devilish atheism and tries to bring him to repentance. Finding the Friar proof against sophistry, Giovanni throws religion and convention aside, and begs the consent of his sister. She sadly confesses that she has long felt the same desire for him. They yield to their sinful passion.

Annabella has been scorning all the suitors approved by her father: Grimaldi, a soldier, Soranzo, a nobleman, and Bergetto, the simpleton son of Donado. But when she becomes pregnant, she submits to her father's wishes and consents to marry Soranzo and cleave to him. The lovers hope that fear of public disgrace will make the deceived husband conceal his wife's shame. But as soon as Soranzo discovers her condition, he flies into a rage of vituperation and insult, and sets his servant Velasco to discover who is the father of her child. When this is accomplished, through confession of Annabella's nurse Putana, he invites Florio's entire family along with other citizens to a state dinner in honour of the Cardinal, at which he proposes to have public revenge upon Giovanni. But Giovanni anticipates his design; bidding farewell to his sister, who is now bitterly repentant, he stabs her, cuts out her heart, and brings it on dagger-tip to the banquet table. Florio falls dead. Soranzo's paid assassins attack Giovanni, who manages to stab Soranzo to death before he receives his own death blow.

Giovanni is the melancholic of *'Tis Pitty*. His ailment is gradually and unobtrusively introduced. Few will notice that in the first scene of the play the Friar has called Giovanni, half-seriously, "foolish madman."[1] His melancholy begins to be marked in the second and third scenes, now that he has tried the Friar's regimen and it has failed: Annabella and Putana both notice and remark upon his sadness:

> *Anna.* Sure 'tis not hee; this is some woefull thinge
> Wrapt up in griefe, some shaddow of a man.[2]

[1] *'Tis Pitty*, I, i (Sherman, p. 6). The warning is repeated, II, v (Sherman, p. 46).
[2] *ibid.*, I, ii (Sherman, p. 15).

Anna.   Howsoever I am, me thinks you are not well.
[*To Gio.*
Putana   Blesse us! why are you so sad, sir?[3]

His conversation is by bursts, ill-connected and ominous, so
that Annabella fears lest he be "franticke."[4] He admits that he
is sick to death, and the fact that he seems to be satirical leads
Annabella to conclude that he has the "merry sicknesse"[5]—that
he has melancholy caused by blood adust, in which the patient
is given to wit and the company of women. Giovanni's father
Florio, notices his sickness and ascribes it to too much study:

You see I have but two, a sonne and her;
And hee is so devoted to his booke,
As I must tell you true, I doubt his health;[6]

on another occasion to solitariness:

Sonne, where have you beene? What, alone, alone, still, still?
I would not have it so; you must forsake
This over bookish humour;[7]

both are certain causes of melancholy.

Annabella's diagnosis of "merry melancholy" is incorrect.
So is Florio's of "student's melancholy." Actually Giovanni
is afflicted with religious melancholy in defect. He is a learned
and thoughtful youth. Before he went to the university and
while he was there, his belief was so whole as to be completely
satisfactory to his devout Friar, and everybody applauded his
"goverment, behaviour, learning, speech, Sweetnesse, and all
that could make up a man."[8] But since his return he has developed this unlawful passion for his sister. Perceiving that his
desires are out of accord with his old belief, he tries to under-
mine the justice of that belief. His intellectual struggle through
the five acts is an attempt to establish the rule of "fate" (or
"fortune" in Burton's phrase) and "nature" as against the
rule of God: before the opening of the first scene he has been

---

[3] *ibid.,* I, iii (Sherman, p. 17).
[5] *ibid.*
[7] *ibid.,* II, vi (Sherman, p. 54).

[4] *ibid.* (Sherman, p. 18).
[6] *ibid.,* I, iv (Sherman, p. 22).
[8] *ibid.,* I, i (Sherman, p. 7).

trying by atheistic arguments to prove that there is no God, a position which the Friar flatly condemns, for

> nice philosophy
> May tolerate unlikely arguments,
> But heaven admits no'jest; wits that presum'd
> On wit too much,—by striving how to prove
> There was no God,—with foolish grounds of art
> Discover'd first the neerest way to hell,
> And fild the world with develish atheisme.[9]

The Friar warns the unhappy youth of the only possible prognosis of atheism: the damnation of his soul,[10] and eloquently recommends the only possible cure: repentance—good Burtonian doctrine as well as Churchly:

> Hye to thy fathers house, there locke thee fast
> Alone within thy chamber, then fall downe
> On both thy knees, and grovell on the ground:
> Cry to thy heart, wash every word thou utter'st
> In teares,—and if't bee possible,—of blood:
> Begge heaven to cleanse the leprosie of lust
> That rots thy soule, acknowledge what thou art,
> A wretch, a worme, a nothing.[11]

Giovanni faithfully follows these commands and tries to save himself. When he next appears (I, iii), the rule of God seems for a fleeting instant predominant, as he cries out "lost," "death," "ruine." But actually the rule of fate has won:

> tis not, I know,
> My lust, but 'tis my fate that leads me on.[12]

This triumph of atheism is the seal of his melancholy. Now that his mind is distempered, for the first time he acts upon his passion for his sister.

When the deed is committed, a feeling of uncertainty brings him again to the Friar (II, v): he feels he must convince his advisor before conviction will be complete in his own mind; but "nature" is now really predominant: "What I have done

[9] *ibid.* (Sherman, p. 5).
[10] *ibid.* (Sherman, p. 7).
[11] *ibid.* (Sherman, p. 8).
[12] *ibid.*, I, iii (Sherman, p. 16).

I'le prove both fit and good,"[13] he says confidently, as he introduces his argument from Platonism:

> It is a principall, which you have taught
> When I was yet your scholler, that the f[r]ame
> And composition of the minde doth follow
> The frame and composition of body:
> So, where the bodies furniture is beauty,
> The mindes must needs be vertue;
>
> .   .   .   .   .
>
> .   .   .   . this proves
> My sisters beauty being rarely faire
> Is rarely vertuous; chiefely in her love,
> And chiefely in that love, her love to me.[14]

The reason for this considerable increase in confidence is rooted
in the individual experience of the man: since he has experienced
his sister, he knows a love so profound that he thinks his soul
well lost for it. His view is now exactly that of Burton's
hedonist:

> Let poaring booke-men dreame of other worlds;
> My world and all of happinesse is here,
> And I'de not change it for the best to come:—
> A life of pleasure in Elyzeum.[15]

Again, whereas formerly he stood alone in his rebellion against
the law of God, now he has the strength of corroboration
"She is like mee, and I like her, resolv'd."[16] They have "given
themselves over to wantoness."

At length (V, iii), through indulgence Giovanni does cauter-
ize his conscience:

> *Fryar*   Thy conscience, youth, is sear'd;
> Else thou wouldst stoope to warning,[17]

until, with Burton's atheist, he laughs at the Friar for being
a superstitious fool:

> The hell you oft have prompted is nought else
> But slavish and fond superstitious feare.[18]

[13] *ibid.*, II, v (Sherman, p. 45).   [14] *ibid.* (Sherman, pp. 45-6).
[15] *ibid.*, V, iii (Sherman, p. 105).   [16] *ibid.*, II, v (Sherman, p. 48).
[17] *ibid.*, V, iii (Sherman, p. 106).   [18] *ibid.*

Then Giovanni's confidence receives a severe shock as the shades begin to close around him: his friend the Friar deserts him in horror and departs for Bononia, leaving Giovanni "to despayre." And Giovanni might well have taken this path, even as did Malefort in Massinger's *The Unnatural Combat*. Ford chose rather to keep his hero's character consistently along one line of religious melancholy in defect: he is still "secure, void of grace and fears." "Despaire or tortures of a thousand hells, All's one to mee,"[19] he says. Desolate now, he turns to his last remaining friend, the partner of his sin (V, v). While still asserting his disbelief in immortality, he wants desperately to believe in it for a new reason: now that he has made up his mind to kill Annabella, he cannot endure to think of eternal separation from her:

> *Gio.* The schoole-men teach that all this globe of earth
> Shalbe consum'd to ashes in a minute.
> *Anna.* So I have read too.
> *Gio.* But 'twere somewhat strange
> To see the waters burne: could I beleeve
> This might be true, I could beleeve as well
> There might be hell or heaven.
> *Anna.* That's most certaine.
> *Gio.* A dreame, a dreame! else in this other world
> Wee should know one another.
> *Anna.* So wee shall.
> *Gio.* Have you heard so?
> *Anna.* For certaine.[20]

Accordingly in their last moments he sets up a double standard of belief: Christian heaven for her:

> Goe thou, white in thy soule, to fill a throne
> Of innocence and sanctity in heaven,[21]

a problematical after-life for himself:

> Oh, my last minute comes!
> Where e're I goe, let mee enjoy this grace,
> Freely to view my Annabella's face.[22]

19 *ibid.* (Sherman, p. 108).
21 *ibid.* (Sherman, p. 116).
20 *ibid.*, V, v (Sherman, p. 114).
22 *ibid.*, V, vi (Sherman, p. 123).

In short, Giovanni in his dying breath is as unrepentant as
he was before Annabella's conception; although his confidence
in "nature" is shaken by the desertion of the Friar and by the
very love which established it in the first place. "Atheism" it
was in the beginning and is now. So it is that Annabella and her
father still read in his face the signs of actual mental aberration:

> *Gio.*   Looke up, looke here; what see you in my face?
> *Anna.*   Distraction and a troubled countenance.[23]

> *Florio*   Why, mad-man, art thy selfe?
> .   .   .   .
> .   .   . How! alas, my lords,
> Hee's a frantick mad-man![24]

So it is that while violating all conventional moralities, Giovanni
can praise his own actions as if he had established a superior
morality, when killing his sister:

> When thou art dead
> I'le give my reasons for't; for to dispute
> With thy—even in thy death—most lovely beauty
> Would make mee stagger to performe *this act*
> *Which I most glory in*;[25]

when killing Soranzo:

> *For in my fists I beare the twists of life.*
> Soranzo, see this heart which was thy wives;
> Thus I exchange it royally for thine; [*Stabs him.*][26]

even in his own death:

> *Cardinal*   Thinke on thy life and end, and call for mercy.
> *Gio.*   Mercy? why I have found it in *this justice.*[27]

PERKIN WARBECK

Perkin Warbeck is the story of a pretender to the English
crown during the reign of Henry VII. With the assertion
that he was Richard, the younger of the two little sons of
Edward IV, whom Richard III murdered in the Tower, he

---

[23] *ibid.*, V, v (Sherman, p. 115).   [24] *ibid.*, V, vi (Sherman, p. 120).
[25] *ibid.*, V, v (Sherman, p. 117). Italics mine.
[26] *ibid.*, V, vi (Sherman, p. 122). Italics mine.
[27] *ibid.* (Sherman, p. 123). Italics mine.

won the support of Charles VIII of France and of Edward IV's sister, Margaret Duchess of Burgundy. After several unsuccessful attempts to raise a rebellion in England, in Ford's play he convinces young King James of Scotland of the justice of his claims. James gives his cousin Katherine Gordon to Warbeck in marriage, although she was already betrothed to Lord Dalyell, and leads the Scotch forces against King Henry. The English are everywhere victorious. When, through the clever diplomacy of Hialas, Henry's Spanish-born special ambassador to Scotland, James is led to abandon Warbeck's cause, the Pretender moves his campaign to the South. Joining forces with the Cornish, who are already in rebellion, he prepares to meet the English at Taunton. But growing faint at heart at the last moment, he flees from the battle. Captured shortly after by Lord Dawbeney, he is tried, found guilty of treason, and executed on Tower Hill, still proclaiming that he is a true-born Plantagenet.

The central character of *Perkin Warbeck* is not a melancholic, for he lacks the requisite fear and sadness; and he is not dependent upon any specific Burtonian type. Yet he is a fellow to Ford's melancholy characters: he suffers from the confirmed delusion that he is somebody else:

> The custom, sure, of being styl'd a king
> Hath fasten'd in his thought that he is such.[1]

His own story is that after the hired murderers had killed his brother Edward,

> The softness of my childhood smil'd upon
> The roughness of their task, and robb'd them farther
> Of hearts to dare, or hands to execute;[2]

that he was then secretly conveyed to Tournay, where he grew up in obscurity; until,

> recollecting who I was, I shook off
> My bondage, and made haste to let my aunt
> Of Burgundy acknowledge me her kinsman,
> Heir to the crown of England.[3]

[1] *Perkin Warbeck*, V, ii (Bullen, II, 206).
[2] *ibid.*, II, i (Bullen, II, 140).   [3] *ibid.*

He lives this part with conviction. King James is impressed with his kingly utterance[4] and bearing,[5] and even King Henry, who is utterly skeptical, is surprised at his fine and polished behaviour even after disastrous reverses.[6] He never falters in the part even in his private relations and in the face of death.

But his enemies have a different story of Warbeck's origins: he was born in Tournay, son of a renegade Jew named Osbeck, who turned Christian to mend his fortunes.[7] When he was grown to manhood, his pretentions were used as a tool by a succession of trouble-makers, among them the Geraldines and Butlers of Ireland, and King Charles of France.[8] Now nourished on the malice of the old Duchess of Burgundy, and backed by King James of Scotland, he is come once again to make his preposterous claim upon the throne of England.[9] In the opinion of the English court, Margaret is a sort of sorceress (such as causes Burtonian melancholy) and her influence upon the traitorous Clifford as well as upon Warbeck is witchcraft, magic, charms, and incantations.[10] She made Warbeck's pretence take root in his own mind, repeated the story so frequently that it was transformed into truth:

> A pretty gallant! Thus, your aunt of Burgundy,
> Your duchess-aunt, inform'd her nephew; so,
> The lesson prompted and well conn'd, was moulded
> Into familiar dialogue, oft rehears'd,
> Till, learnt by heart, 'tis now receiv'd for truth.[11]

Some hold the opinion that Warbeck has learned witchcraft too, and by that power has deluded James and won the heart of the court beauty, Katherine Gordon,[12]

Holding this opinion and finding Warbeck confirmed in his assertions, the English perforce conclude that he is mad: Henry sends him and his followers to the Tower with the hope that

> Time may restore their wits, whom vain ambition
> Hath many years distracted.[13]

[4] *ibid.* (Bullen, II, 141).
[5] *ibid.*, II, iii (Bullen, II, 152).
[6] *ibid.*, V, ii (Bullen, II, 203).
[7] *ibid.*, V, iii (Bullen, II, 209).
[8] *ibid.*, I, i (Bullen, II, 121).
[9] *ibid.*, II, ii (Bullen, II, 148).
[10] *ibid.*, I, iii (Bullen, II, 131).
[11] *ibid.*, V, ii (Bullen, II, 204).
[12] *ibid.*, II, iii (Bullen, II, 148-9); III, i (Bullen, II, 157-8).
[13] *ibid.*, V, ii (Bullen, II, 206).

When Warbeck has been tried and condemned to death and is
on the way to the scaffold, he is confronted with Lambert
Simnel, the other famous pretender to the throne of Henry VII,
who claimed to be Edward, Earl of Warwick, son of the Duke
of Clarence. Simnel relates the story of his confession, and
recommends that Warbeck too admit that he is a mere rascal.
Warbeck scornfully and majestically repulses the suggestion;
whereupon Simnel says

> He's past
> Recovery; a Bedlam cannot cure him.[14]

And Surrey recommends him to eternity with

> Prepare your journey
> To a new kingdom, then, unhappy madman,
> Wilfully foolish.[15]

The real Warbeck may have been only a consummate imposter;
Ford's is not: he seals with his brave death the warrant that he
truly believes he is Duke Richard of York. Fully deluded, he is
worthy of pity as well as of death:

> *Dawbeney*   I here present you, royal sir, a shadow
> Of majesty, but in effect a substance
> Of pity.[16]

THE QUEEN

"An excellent old Play" called *The Queen, or The Excellency
of Her Sex* was found by a "Person of Honour" some years
after the probable death of Ford and given to the publisher
Alexander Goughe [Goffe], who printed it in London some-
time before August 13, 1653.[1] Goughe did not know the identity
of its author, and none of the makers of seventeenth-century
Play Lists—Rogers and Ley (1656), Archer (1656), Kirkman

---

[14] *ibid.*, V, iii (Bullen, II, 211).   [15] *ibid.* (Bullen, II, 214).

[16] *ibid.*, V, ii (Bullen, II, 203). An interpretation of *Perkin Warbeck* from
the point of view of modern psychology will be found in Lawrence Babb's
"Abnormal Psychology in John Ford's *Perkin Warbeck*," *Modern Language
Notes*, LI (1936), 234-7.

[1] The date under which it appears in the record book of George Thomason,
collector of Commonwealth tracts and friends of John Milton. See Thomason,
Catalogue, II, 33.

(1661)—ventured a guess.[2] For more than two centuries after that time the play remained anonymous. Then in 1908 W. Bang republished it as Vol. XIII of the *Materialien zur Kunde des älteren Englischen Dramas,* ascribing it to John Ford on the grounds of similarity to Ford's known works in six respects: 1) action of the main characters, 2) juxtaposition of poetically elevated passages with tasteless and low comedy ones, 3) character drawing, 4) ideas, 5) hyperbolical style, 6) vocabulary.[3] Sherman, in a review of Bang's edition, corroborated his ascription.[4] The absence of a single attempt to question the soundness of this judgment leaves Ford in undisputed possession of the field, in spite of the fact that there has not been discovered one item of external evidence to support it. Consequently the following pages treat *The Queen* as an established item in the Ford canon.

The principal action of *The Queen* deals with the cure of a king's distraction. Alphonso, a melancholic misogynist, leads a seditious rebellion against the crown of Arragon. He is condemned to death. The Queen, however, falls in love with him, and offers him a reprieve and her hand in marriage as he mounts the scaffold. All she asks in return is love. After the wedding is solemnized and Alphonso is proclaimed king, his first act is to banish the Queen from his bed for a week. It soon appears that he means to extend this banishment indefinitely, for, when a month has passed, he still forbids her his company and grows ever more censorious of her sex. The king's friend, Muretto, then undertakes cure of the melancholy, even though his services have been scornfully rejected by the Queen's favourite Petruchi. First poisoning the king's mind with the suspicion of improper relations between Petruchi and the Queen, he brings Alphonso at the same time to an examination of the Queen's beauty. Before long Alphonso openly accuses her of adultery and provides that her honour will be tried by combat: if in a month's time a champion for her appears, the king himself will meet him; if not, she loses her head. Proceeding the while

[2] See Greg, Appendix II, p. ci.   [3] *The Queen,* pp. vii-viii.
[4] Sherman, "A New Play by John Ford," *Modern Language Notes,* XXIII (1908), 245-9.

with his treatment, Muretto has now brought the king from misogyny through jealousy to love; so that when the day of the trial arrives, Alphonso feels that whether he kills or dies in the fight, he will be vanquished. Three champions for the Queen appear: Velasco, her general, Petruchi, her favourite and supposed paramour, and Muretto. Before the combat can actually begin, Muretto reveals that he alone is responsible for the jeopardy in which the Queen's honour now stands; that he strove thus to supplant misogyny in the king's mind with the contrary emotions of jealousy and love. All are convinced of the Queen's innocence, Muretto is commended, Alphonso takes the Queen to his arms, and all ends happily.

Alphonso is the only melancholic of *The Queen*. His affliction is not explained in the customary lengthy initial description, but is commented upon by many characters. Petruchi, an important young lord of the court, finds the king "distracted";[5] Almado, a counsellor, "drown'd In melancholy and sowre discontent";[6] the Queen says he looks "sadly."[7] Pynto, the court astronomer who "scientifically" predicts every major turn of events in the play, gives us the key to the cause of Alphonso's melancholy: "Here's a high Saturnal spirit,"[8] he exclaims as the king goes to execution captious and stubborn. Alphonso is melancholy, then, as a result of the maleficent influence of the stars—a sufficient cause in itself Burton says. Every detail of his behaviour will be found to be a consistent exemplification of Saturnine characteristics. And, finally, Muretto, the king's truest friend, states that he suffers from a "distraction" caused by his "discontents."[9] Muretto goes on, in a speech late in the play, to reveal that the whole course of the action has been under his direction. He is the "physician" who "bent all his studies" to the analysis, treatment and cure of the king's distraction:

Muretto Wonder not my Lords, but lend mee your attentions[.] I saw with what violence he [Alphonso] pursude his resolutions not more in detestation of the Queen in particular,

[5] *The Queen*, (I, i) l. 262.
[7] *ibid.*, (II, ii) l. 1175.
[9] *ibid.*, (V, ii) ll. 3591-2.
[6] *ibid.*, ll. 447-8.
[8] *ibid.*, (I, i) l. 268.

then of all her sex in generall. That I may not weary your
patience: I bent all my Studies to devise, which way I might
do service to my country, by reclayming the distraction of his
discontents. And having felt his disposition in every pulse,
I found him most addicted to this pestilence of jealosy[;]
with a strong persuasion of which I from time to time, ever
fed him by degrees, till I brought the Queen and the noble
Petruchi into the dangers they yet stand in. But with all (and
herin I appeale to your Majesties own approbation) I season'd
my words with such an intermixing the praises of the Queens
bewty, that from jealosy I drew the King into a serious examination of her perfections. . . . At length having found
him indeed surely affected, I perceav'd, that nothing but the
suppos'd blemish of her dishonour, could work a second divorce
between them. . . . Now my Lords, to cleer that imputation,
I knew how easie it would be, by the apparent certainty it
selfe[.] In all which, if I have erred, it is the error of a
loy[a]ll service. Only I must ever acknowledg how justly I
have deserved a punishment, in drawing so vertuous a prin-
cesses honor into publick question; and humbly referr my selfe
to her gracious clemency, and your noble constructions.[10]

This is a strikingly literal application of Burton's statement
of the offices of friendship in the cure of melancholy. Here are
Burton's words:

If his weakness be such, that he cannot discern what is amiss,
correct or satisfy, it behoves them [his friends] by counsel,
comfort, or persuasion, by fair or foul means, to alienate his
mind, by some artificial invention, or some contrary persuasion,
to remove all objects, causes, companies, occasions, as may
anyways molest him, to humour him, please him, divert him,
and, if it be possible, by altering his course of life, to give him
security and satisfaction. If he conceal his grievances, and
will not be known of them, *they must observe by his looks,
gestures, motions, phantasy, what it is that offends*, and then
to apply remedies unto him. Many are instantly cured, when
their minds are satisfied.[11]

Following these two statements of the plan we may observe, in
the action, Alphonso's Saturnine traits and Muretto's scheme
of treatment and cure.

---

[10] *ibid.*, ll. 3583-624.   [11] Burton, II, 126.

The first named and most obvious trait is his hatred of womankind in general and of the Queen in particular:

> I hate your sex in general, not you
> As y'are a Queen, but as y'are a woman.[12]

This misogyny needs no further demonstration to anyone who will glance at the text. It is the main theme of the play, constantly reiterated and steadily intensified throughout the first two acts.[13] As a Saturnine "contemner of women" he is "ever repining." Having quietly observed this in the first act, Muretto is already, in Act II, Scene ii, "bending all his studies to feel the king's disposition in every pulse," observing "by his looks, gestures, motions, phantasy, what it is that offends." He allows himself to seem the most stupid (or the most parasitical)[14] of mortals, in order to insinuate himself securely into the confidence of the king and thus catch him in his natural disposition. He agrees with everything Alphonso may say; for instance, a true king should not yield to entreaties if it is not his will to yield.[15] This is Saturnine stubbornness. The Queen comes, to plead her own cause, and, after getting much the better of her lord in a brief argument, hears herself accused of fickleness in love. "Is that your fear?" she asks; then turning to her own supporters:

> Why la now, Lords, I told you that the King
> Made our division but a proof of faith.
> Kinde husband, now I'm bold to call you so;
> Was this your cunning to be jealous of me
> So soon?[16]

Muretto is evidently already satisfied that the king is "most addicted to this pestilence of jealosy," as he says aside to the spectators:

> You'l scarce find it so;[17]

that is, You (the Queen) will scarce find that his jealousy is cunning only. With this nail he will force out the Saturnine

---

[12] *The Queen*, (I, i) ll. 386-7.
[13] Note especially *ibid.*, ll. 247-61, 265-6, 338-51, 362-70, 380-93, 400-31, 651-60, 674-9, 1046-50, 1143-5, 1181-94, 1200-11, 1214-36.
[14] *ibid.*, (II, ii) ll. 1312-14. [15] *ibid.*, ll. 1030-3.
[16] *ibid.*, ll. 1161-9. [17] *ibid.*, l. 1171.

melancholy. The wrathful outburst which follows, and during which Muretto is the silent observer, expands the theme of violent jealousy.[18] After Alphonso has gone off with a vehement parting shot, Muretto remains to hear what the Queen will say and to give her the comfort that can be derived from his certainty in his own control of the situation:

> If your excellent Majesty please to repose confidence in me;
> I will not onely deliver him your commendations, but think
> my self highly dishonored, if he return not his back to you by
> letter.[19]

As the third act opens, Muretto has already begun his treatment ("I season'd my words with . . . an intermixing the praises of the Queens bewty") with such success that Alphonso is now willing to acknowledge his gratitude to, and love for, the Queen.[20] He calls her virtuous and asks to be commended to her as so believing. Muretto is delighted, but, though he thinks himself to be wholly in the king's confidence, he is as yet merely another of the king's dupes, for the latter confides to his audience in a soliloquy,

> Henceforth my Stratagem's of scorn and hatred
> Shall kill in smiles. I will not strike and frown,
> But laugh and murther.[21]

This tendency to dissemble is characteristic of Saturnine melancholy. Unsuspecting, however, Muretto continues his treatment ("with a strong persuasion of [jealousy] I from time to time, ever fed him by degrees, till I brought the Queen and the noble Petruchi into the dangers they yet stand in"): with words strongly reminiscent both of *Loves Sacrifice* and *Othello*,[22] he leads Alphonso to suspect the Queen of adultery

---

18 *ibid.*, ll. 1215-26.   19 *ibid.*, ll. 1300-5.
20 *ibid.*, (III, i) ll. 1542-50.
21 *ibid.*, ll. 1596-600.
22 Note especially these parallels:
    The Queen, (III, i) ll. 1630-1:
        "*Muret.* But what of all this? There might be no harm meant."
    Othello, IV, i (Oxford, p. 908):
        "*Iago* . . . not meaning any harm."
    The Queen, (III, i) l. 1651:
        "*Alph.* Canst prove that?"

with Petruchi. Having developed this suspicion into an active conviction, Muretto allows his scheme to mark time while he awaits further developments.

These come rapidly enough (III, ii). Alphonso sends Muretto with a letter of reconciliation to the Queen and a ring (which was the gift of the Queen) to Petruchi. The Queen, recognizing the ring and being animated with renewed love and gratitude, begs that she may have it in exchange for the one she wears:

> *Qu.* How! 'Tis my ring,
> The first ring that I ever gave the King.
> *Petruchi,* I must have it.
> *Petr.* 'Twas the King sent it:
> *I* mean to yeeld it back again.
> *Qu.* No I will.
> And in exchange take that of equal value;
> But not with me, 'cause it comes from my husband.[23]

Muretto remains with her party as they go to greet the king (III, iii), not knowing that in the meantime Alphonso has made plans for the apprehension of Petruchi and the Queen on charges of treason and adultery. The king seizes with gleeful rage upon the fact that their rings have been exchanged, regarding it as sufficient proof without further argument that they are guilty. Muretto is a silent observer of this final proof of

Othello, III, iii (Oxford, p. 899):
> "*Othello* Villain, be sure thou prove my love a whore,
> Be sure of it."

The Queen, (III, i) ll. 1665-6:
> "*Muret.* Yet faith, let me perswade ye; I hope your wife is vertuous."

Othello, III, iii (Oxford, p. 901):
> "*Iago* Nay, but be wise; yet we see nothing done;
> She may be honest yet."

The Queen, (III, i) ll. 1671-5:
> "*Muret.* Why not Sir? I think now a woman may lie four or five nights together with a man, and yet be chast; though that be very hard, yet so long as 'tis possible, such a thing may be."

Othello, IV, i (Oxford, p. 908):
> "*Iago* Or to be naked with her friend a-bed
> An hour or more . . .
> If they do nothing, 'tis a venial slip."

[23] *The Queen,* (III, ii) ll. 2015-25.

Alphonso's jealousy. It is the salvation of his design that summary justice is not executed upon the offending pair, but that
the Queen's honour is to be defended in tournament and that
a month is to be allowed for her to find a champion. During
this month Muretto will have time to proceed with his plan
and accordingly to bring Alphonso "from jealousy . . . into a
serious examination of her perfections." With this second nail
(love) he will drive out the Saturnine melancholy.

In Act IV, Scene i, he undertakes this charge, praising the
Queen in superlative terms[24] and drawing the king into assent.[25]
He informs the king that his greatest sin was his failure to
bring this beauty to its full fruition,[26] even excusing Petruchi
his (supposed) attack upon the Queen's virtue, because "his
nobleness is eternal . . . in injoying the glory of his time, a
beau[ty] so conquering, so unparalell'd."[27] When the king in-
sists she must die if none defend her, Muretto agrees as cour-
teously as the king has agreed with him, but again skillfully
turns the thought back to her beauty: " 'Tis a heroical disposition. . . . If she live and you receive her to favour, you will
be a noted Cuckold. . . . On the other side, if you prevail, and
she be put to death, you do as it were deprive the Firma[m]ent
of the Sun, and your self of the treasure of the whole earth."[28]
Alphonso has learned his lesson well, for he is deeply affected
by the suggestion both of jealousy and affection, and now trusts
his friend in any direction the latter may choose to lead his
thoughts. The balance is now quite equal between the two ideas:

> *Alph.*   My Queen might live now though I did but look
> And gaze upon her cheeks, her ravishing cheeks.
> But, oh, to be a Cuckold; 's death, she dyes,[29]

and Muretto therefore brings the three characters together in
the fine "Basilisk-scene" (IV, ii). Muretto is as good a Burtonian as his predecessor Rhetias in that he brings Alphonso
under the direct influence of the Queen's *eyes*, for the passion
of love is more swiftly and powerfully produced by them than
by any other means, says Burton. The Queen and Petruchi are

[24] *ibid.*, (IV, ii) ll. 2383-4.
[26] *ibid.*, ll. 2424-5.
[28] *ibid.*, ll. 2472-82.

[25] *ibid.*, ll. 2411-13.
[27] *ibid.*, ll. 2435-8.
[29] *ibid.*, ll. 2499-504.

made to sit at opposite sides of the stage where the king (standing between them) can see but one at a time. They symbolize
the two passions which distract his mind: the Queen, love;
Petruchi, jealousy—or, as Alphonso names them: the Queen,
his "comforts"; Petruchi, his "shame."[30] As he looks from one
to the other, his disposition is swayed back and forth. At length
he is ready to forgive the Queen, even while convinced of her
guilt, but the intolerable thought of leaving her beauty behind
him to be enjoyed by another when he dies—the enviousness
of Saturnine melancholy—prevents this rash conclusion. He
orders the two (supposed) offenders off, refusing to believe
their repeated assurances of innocence. This is the final scene
in Muretto's treatment of the king, showing him successful in
achieving the balance of passion which is to cure Alphonso's
melancholy and for which Muretto has been laboring so dili-
gently. "This is admirable," he says, "all my business ripens
to my wishes."[31] Returning to Muretto's revelation, we find
that the action has now reached the point where he could say,
"At length having found him indeed surely affected, I perceav'd, that nothing but the suppos'd blemish of her dishonour,
could work a second divorce between them." That is, he was
so deeply in love that, granting the clearing of her character, the
melancholy passions would have been driven out and they would
live in accord thereafter.

Confident of the truth of this idea, Muretto permits the
preparations for the tournament to progress as planned, in the
second scene of Act V, still playing upon the power he has
observed the Queen's eyes have over Alphonso.[32] The king, in
fact, is so well tutored that, just before the trumpet announcing
the approach of the champions sounds, he asks that he be placed
where he can derive "double strength from her sweet beauty."[33]
When the champions have appeared and the trial by conflict
is about to begin, Muretto makes his revelations. These give
Alphonso security and satisfaction, bring about the mutual for-

[30] *ibid.*, ll. 2534-5. [31] *ibid.*, ll. 2677-9.
[32] *ibid.*, (V, ii) ll. 3355-63.
[33] *ibid.*, ll. 3420-21. Ford's general indebtedness to Burton in *The Queen*
was first remarked by W. Bang in the notes to his edition of the play.

giveness of all, and secure the happy conclusion to a situation which seemed to offer nothing but tragedy. The whole difference between this play as comedy and as tragedy lies in the friendship of Muretto and his benevolent ministrations.

The Ladies Triall tells once again the story of suspicion of a wife's virtue. Auria, a noble Genoese, in an attempt to restore his fortunes, goes to join the Duke of Florence in a raid on Turkish pirates, leaving his recent bride Spinella in the protection of his friend Aurelio. During her husband's absence Spinella is so unwise as to visit Adurni, a free-living young lord, and to allow herself to be received in his bedroom. Adurni locks the door on her and makes an unsuccessful attempt on her virtue. This is the first trial in the play. Aurelio, seriously active in his duty, breaks in upon them, jumps to the conclusion that Spinella has yielded to Adurni, and so reports to Auria when the husband returns. Spinella, insulted at the suspicion, takes refuge, secretly, in the home of her sister Castanna.

The rest of the play is taken up largely with three long scenes like trials at law, with charges, witnesses, testimony and verdict, in which Auria undertakes, with conscious attempt to keep reason dominant over passion, to ascertain the truth about Adurni and Spinella. The first is the trial of Aurelio's good faith. Aurelio repeats his charge, basing it upon two facts, the locked door, and Spinella's guilty-looking flight. Auria at length is satisfied with the purity of Aurelio's motives but still blames his rash suspicion for itself casting the shadow upon Spinella's virtue. The second trial investigates Adurni's guilt. Adurni freely admits his attempt but clings to the assertion that Spinella proved a good woman. At length Auria decides that Adurni, too, is a man of credit. This scarcely settles the question, however, for the two honourable men give contrary testimony. We come therefore to the final trial, the investigation of Spinella's guilt. Her defence is in fact no defence: proudly resting upon her injured innocence, she refuses to make plea for pity or mercy as long as there is the most trifling charge against her. Actually nobody has succeeded in establishing the strong presumption of guilt necessary for a trial at law. Her cousin Malfato then enters the lists and turns the action against the prosecution by demanding satisfaction at arms for the injury to Spinella's name—another trial. Auria chooses this moment of climax to announce that he is satisfied—to rule, in effect, that no true bill has been found. The play closes as he takes Spinella back to his arms.

Malfato is the only melancholic of *The Ladies Triall*. We learn of his affliction incidentally, through Aurelio's questions (I, iii). Animated by the desire to help Malfato, Aurelio states that an habitual melancholy is likely to be the result of love or strong discontents; and suggests that Malfato confide his grief in a friend:

> A melancholy grounded and resolv'd,
> Receiv'd into a habit, argues love,
> Or deep impression of strong discontents.
> In cases of these rarities a friend,
> Upon whose faith and confidence we may
> Vent with security our grief, becomes
> Oft-times the best physician ;[1]

for even if cure does not come from the advice of the friend, at least comfort may result from the unburdening of secret distresses :

> for, admit
> We find no remedy, we cannot miss
> Advice instead of comfort ; and believe
> It is an ease, Malfato, to disburthen
> Our souls of secret clogs, where they may find
> A rest in pity, though not in redress.[2]

Almost the only difference between these ideas and Burton's statement of the use of friendship in the cure of melancholy is that this is in blank verse.

At the end of the scene Malfato is invited into the subplot of Levidolche's light-heeled amours, but he proudly refuses to be a husband "for a cast-suit of bawdry" ;[3] and thereafter has only an absent part in her affairs. When next he appears in his

---

[1] *The Ladies Triall*, I, iii (Bullen, III, 23).
[2] *ibid.* (Bullen, III, 23-4). [3] *ibid.* (Bullen, III, 26).

rightful place in the main plot (IV, i), he is acting upon
Aurelio's advice to unburden himself to a friend. As his con-
fidante he chooses the lady who is also his love, Spinella. Using
a poetic device like Rhetias's in *The Lovers Melancholy*, Malfato tells the romantic story of a kinsman of Spinella's (himself, of course) who falls in love with her, but restrained by the
nearness of their bloods, never speaks of love to her:

> Listen
> To a strange tale, which thus the author sigh'd.
> A kinsman of Spinella,—so it runs,—
> Her father's sister's son, some time before
> Auria, the fortunate, possess'd her beauties,
> Became enamour'd of such rare perfections
> As she was stor'd with; fed his idle hopes
> With possibilities of lawful conquest;
> Found in the argument one only flaw
> Of conscience, by the nearness of their bloods,—
> Unhappy scruple, easily dispens'd with,
> Had any friend's advice resolv'd the doubt.
> Still on he lov'd and lov'd, and wish'd and wish'd.[4]

When she was married to Auria and his hopes permanently
disappointed, he swallowed his grief as best he could, and vowed
never to unlock his secret, never even to come into her presence:

> After her marriage, when remain'd not aught
> Of expectation to such fruitless dotage,
> His reason then,—now,—then—could not reduce
> The violence of passion, though he vow'd
> Ne'er to unlock that secret, scarce to her,
> Herself, Spinella; and withal resolv'd
> Not to come near her presence, but t'avoid
> All opportunities, however proffer'd.[5]

Now he is content with the small good fortune of having the
chance to speak for her good name:

> Then I am thankful for [th'] advantage; urg'd
> By fatal and enjoin'd necessity
> To stand up in defence of injur'd virtue;[6]

---

[4] *ibid.*, IV, i (Bullen, III, 65).   [5] *ibid.* (Bullen, III, 66).
[6] *ibid.*

and hopes by his confession to a friend to have stilled the
tempest of his melancholy:

> I'll bless that hand,
> Whose honourable pity seals the passport
> For my incessant turmoils to their rest.[7]

Malfato makes the chance to do as he offered when he speaks
nobly in defence of Spinella's virtue in the final scene. That is
all there is to his small and delicately drawn part in the play.

Malfato suffers, then, from true Burtonian love-melancholy,
to which there is no cure, since the lady has made another
choice; but he avails himself of what solace there is in Burton's
advice to impart his troubles to a discreet, trusty, loving friend.

[7] *ibid.*

III

THE SIGNIFICANCE OF MELANCHOLY

THE range of Ford's interest in melancholy is the whole of Burton's treatise and more. As we advance through his plays, we view a gallery of melancholy types representing almost every major type in *The Anatomy*. Each new play presents a new one, distinguished from all the others by differences in causes—as Burton's are distinguished: Palador and Meleander illustrate melancholy resulting from great grief, shame and disgrace, discontents, and loss of liberty; Octavio, jealous melancholy caused by impotence; Bassanes, the standard jealous melancholy, caused by the beauty of his wife, his ugliness, her youth, his age, the presence of temptation, and his own excessive love; Ithocles, melancholy caused by ambition; Philippo, jealous melancholy caused by the same things which caused Bassanes's but with the addition of the fact that he was already melancholy; Giovanni, religious melancholy in defect; Warbeck, delusion caused by witchcraft (not specifically treated by Burton); Alphonso, melancholy caused by the influence of the stars; Malfato, love-melancholy. An almost inexhaustible store of other types remained in the pages of Burton ready to be dramatized. Whatever be the reason that Ford wrote no more, it was not exhaustion of the vein; nor was it loss of interest after ten long years (1628-1638) of preoccupation with the subject, for even *The Ladies Triall* shows by both positive and negative evidence the perennial freshness of the subject.

FORD'S ACCURACY

Even from the very beginning of his work on the subject, Ford's comprehension of his material is scientific and exact. All around him in the drama there was an indiscriminate confusion of melancholy and madness. But using Burton's measuring instruments, he cut his material cleanly. It is laid down that madness is without all fear and sadness. So when Meleander goes mad from time to time, he is "insensible of cares"; madness enables Penthea to talk a language which is sad to the hearers but a happy release from stress for her; the fears and cares which would crush a healthy man are cast lightly aside by Warbeck, Ford's only consistently mad man. It is laid down, at the other end of the scale, that melancholy in disposition is sadness proportional to the causes and that it comes and goes. Without exception all the melancholy characters have categorically different traits from these. They are sad beyond the cause, or oversad, and are chronically afflicted. They are bound, whether passive or struggling, in the spell of an enchanted grief.

FORD'S DEVELOPMENT

There is variety and steady progression in Ford's treatment of the subject. Throughout his career he went silently to work on this new and rich scientific theme, ever varying his attack in the attempt to achieve its best dramatic realization. Melancholy first appears in his earliest extant play, *The Witch of Edmonton*, 1621. The Frank Thornay plot, which has generally been ascribed to Ford's hand,[1] presents a character who becomes melancholy as he struggles to find a path through the morass into which his lies and criminal actions have led him. He marries Winnifrede, a servant girl, because he has been tricked into the belief that the child she is soon to bear is his. Then, in order to hold the good will of his father and so to secure his inheritance, he consents to a bigamous marriage with Susan, the girl of his father's choice. With the large dowry that Susan brings, which was to have been used to free the Thornay estate of its encumbrances, he sets out with Winnifrede to flee to "some other nation"[2] where they will be beyond the reach of the law. But the fugitives are overtaken by Susan, and at the instigation of the Devil in the guise of a black dog who rubs against his leg, Frank tries another way out of his difficulty by murdering

---

[1] For authorship of *The Witch of Edmonton*, see Swinburne, "John Ford," *Fortnightly Review*, XVI (1871), 56-7; Gifford (Bullen, III, 196, 212, 220-1, 271-2, notes) ; Fleay, I, 231; Ward, *A History of Dramatic Literature*, II, 470, III, 74-5; Hunt, pp. 178-83; Sargeaunt, pp. 34-41.

[2] *The Witch of Edmonton*, III, ii (Bullen, III, 222).

Susan and directing suspicion against Susan's and her sister's former suitors, Warbeck and Somerton. His crime becomes known through the discovery of his bloody knife, his guilt is established by Winnifrede's testimony, and he is hanged. Again and again in the course of this action Frank shows that the burden of his crime rests heavily upon his mind: Susan observes "strange variations" in him, which are expressed by "sudden and distracted accents" in his sleep;[3] the "hydra of discontent grows rank" in the "fen" of his heart;[4] he is haunted with indefinite fears[5] and with the unlaid ghost of Susan;[6] his fears take physical expression in nausea when he realizes that discovery is impending.[7] These are symptoms of melancholy. But they are not necessarily drawn from Burton. There is as yet no verbal reminiscence. Melancholy is not yet the core of the play, closely analyzed to illuminate the main character and motivate his actions. Instead of this, the poet avoids (rather than welcoming) the problem of a satisfactory psychology for Frank's complex character by shifting the criminal responsibility to the Devil's black dog. The plot is merely the exploitation of a sensational story, no doubt based on real events as well known to the audience as those which furnished the material for Mother Sawyer[8] and for *The Late Murder*.[9]

Raybright in *The Sun's Darling*, 1624, is another melancholy character appearing early in the dramatist's career. In the pages ascribed to Ford by general consent,[10] he shows a "brain disorder'd,"[11] for so the Priest of the Sun decides after hearing Raybright make cynically discontented comments upon his bless-

[3] *ibid.*, II, ii (Bullen, III, 211).

[4] *ibid.* (Bullen, III, 212). See also Bullen, III, 213-15, and 247.

[5] *ibid.*, IV, ii (Bullen, III, 248).   [6] *ibid.* (Bullen, III, 250).

[7] *ibid.* (Bullen, III, 253).

[8] See the prose pamphlet by Henry Goodcole, reprinted in Bullen's edition, I, lxxxi-cvii.

[9] See Sisson, pp. 80-124: *Keep the Widow Waking*, or *The Late Murder in Whitechapel* by Dekker, Rowley, Ford and Webster.

[10] For authorship of *The Sun's Darling*, see Swinburne, "John Ford," *Fortnightly Review*, XVI (1871), 55-6; Gifford (Bullen, III, 169); Fleay, I, 232; Ward, *A History of Dramatic Literature*, II, 470, III, 75; Hunt, pp. 53-4; Sargeaunt, pp. 57-63.

[11] *The Sun's Darling*, I, i (Bullen, III, 112).

ings.[12] The general sense of the play, indeed, though haltingly presented, as if the playwrights were uncertain of their plan, is that Raybright is not long contented with any fortune. At the Sun's direction each of the Seasons in succession bestows her finest gifts upon Raybright; but, although he is happy at first with each beautiful lady, his evil companions Folly and Lady Humour shortly return, bringing with them his old discontent. Lady Humour is the personification of that pampered capriciousness—

> 'Tis melancholy and too fond indulgence
> To your own dull'd affections sway your judgment,[13]

as the Priest says. This serious conception of Raybright's character is in strong contrast with the mere romantic sadness he shows in passages generally assigned to Dekker, such as Act III, Scene i, where he laments the death of Spring. It will be observed, too, that with Dekker Lady Humour has lost her earnest significance and becomes simply the object for jest: Lady Humour is a common creature, common indeed, says Dekker's Raybright, for has not every courtier his Humour, every brave lady hers, every citizen his, every wife hers?[14] Ford's Raybright shows the marks of a deeper interest in melancholy than does Frank Thornay, and the ailment has become the major theme of the play. Moreover, some technical and scientific material concerned with the physiological basis of melancholy has been introduced: the masquers who appear in Act V, Scene i[15] represent the four elements and the four complexions, and they dance together to show the mystic connection between blood and air, choler and fire, etc. The presence of this material suggests that Ford may now have been familiar with at least that part of the *Anatomy* which discusses the humours. But in general his treatment of the subject is still superficial: there is no analysis of the kind of melancholy that afflicts Raybright, no examination of its causes, no attempt at treatment, no solution by either cure or catastrophe. And the masque of the humours might as easily have been drawn from the common

---

[12] *ibid.* (Bullen, III, 110-12).   [13] *ibid.* (Bullen, III, 111).
[14] *ibid.*, III, i (Bullen, III, 135).   [15] Bullen, III, 165.

stock of mediaeval knowledge as from Burton's profound study.

The Lovers Melancholy is a different story. This tragi-comedy demonstrates a detailed acquaintance with the *Anatomy*, as if it had been written in the morning of a fresh enthusiasm. Phrases and ideas, even whole synopses are caught up almost verbatim. The melancholy of the two heroes Palador and Meleander is discussed at great length before they appear, by courtiers, counsellors of state, and physician. They estimate the causes and symptoms, arrive at a diagnosis, prescribe treatment, and effect a cure. Long scenes show the heroes behaving as described, undergoing treatment, and being cured. Not content with these specific studies, the poet extends his field to include a discourse on melancholy in general (by Corax) which embraces, in hasty and sometimes faulty abstract, all of Burton's main divisions: causes, definition, kinds (and here Ford makes direct acknowledgment in a footnote[16] that his source is Burton), parts affected, prognosis, cure, and differentiation from madness. Thereupon he concocts a masque which, in addition to its therapeutic purpose, further exploits Burton's kinds of madness. Unfortunately, in more than one way the presentation is stilted and mechanical; the dramatist is too close to his source; Burton as it were lies open before him. The symptomology sounds like a case history; drama and dialogue and theatrical pretence have to yield to the technique of the classroom as Corax and his too apt pupils expound melancholy by question and answer; the masque naïvely presumes that everybody is interested in the technical aspects of the subject. Playwright and characters are obsessed.

The Fancies, a play which is either much earlier than its date of publication or is the result of a fresh return to the *Anatomy*, shows a novice enthusiasm for Burton only slightly more temperate. The descriptions of Octavio's melancholy and of the surroundings in which he lives are drawn directly from the *Anatomy* and are as copious as those of Palador. Romanello's animadversions on love are as extraneous to character depiction as is the material of the masque in *The Lovers Melancholy*. The

---

[16] *The Lovers Melancholy,* III, i (Bullen, I, 52, n. 5).

treatise, however, is being slowly conned and digested, and can be used with greater originality. The types of Octavio and Romanello are not explicitly outlined in Burton; therefore the material had to be drawn from scattered sections of the *Anatomy*. The play is not entirely preoccupied with the treatment and cure of the melancholics. We hear of the causes, symptoms, and self-initiated treatment of Octavio, but miss him from the stage most of the time. He appears only twice[17] before the denouement, and only once long enough to demonstrate any of his symptoms. No physician applies himself to Octavio's treatment, and the play does not end with his cure, for his ailment and his melancholy are incurable.

With *The Broken Heart* and the three following tragedies we come into the full stream of Ford's mastery of the subject. The dramatist has now assimilated his source material so that he can present it with clarity and conviction in his own words. There is less talk and more action. Bassanes's affliction is analyzed as deeply as Palador's before he appears, with definition, causes, and symptoms, yet with much greater brevity, concentration, assurance. With this business quickly over, a proportionately longer time can be given to the demonstration of his symptoms. Although no physician prescribes for him, he undertakes his own cure by patience, and this phase of his affliction, too, is presented in long scenes of silent suffering. Ithocles's melancholy is drawn with fewer lines, but with equal boldness. We are told before he appears what his melancholy is and what caused it; we see in more than one scene an attempt at treatment in his belated repentance and reformation, and a recurrence of the old failing. In addition the poet has curbed his naïve enthusiasm for the subject for its own sake: there are no more extraneous facts expounded by the pedagogic method of Corax and no more Burtonian aphorisms like Romanello's. The effect is now that of a mysterious uncontrollable plague which blasts the lives of all those who come close to Bassanes and Ithocles.

Loves Sacrifice is an equally mature study of the same problem as that of *The Broken Heart* with some of the counters in

[17] I, i and III, iii.

different positions. Interest is placed in the causes as never before. The initial description of Philippo's plain melancholy before he appears is accidentally fragmentary. Gifford said

> The purport of the lost passage is easily collected from the context. The duke, since his accession, has drawn round him a set of profligate parasites, who, &c. It is scarcely necessary to observe that no part of the duke's conduct justifies the reproach here laid upon him; he is rather a well-meaning dotard, a better Bassanes, than a follower of debauched society: but Ford seems to have lost his way through a great part of this drama.[18]

Judging from the construction of other Ford plays, we know that, on the contrary, this passage analyzed the nature and causes of Philippo's plain melancholy. The inclusion of Ferentes merely shows the lengths to which the duke will go to find solacing companionship and attempt a cure; it does not make him a "follower of debauched society." In thinking that there is inconsistency between description and behaviour, Gifford is the victim of his own mistaken imagination. The loss of the description is of little importance, for we are next offered a choice of causes and a multitude of attempted cures. As in *The Broken Heart*, the material of the treatise is realized more in action than in descriptions. This topic occupies roughly the first three acts of the play. Acts IV and V treat Philippo's second melancholy, jealousy. Its causes in turn are elaborately analyzed and dramatized and its symptoms exhibited in a series of scenes. There is no attempt whatever at treatment of it, and no cure is effected.

'Tis Pitty makes most derivative use of the *Anatomy*. It is more than any other of the plays, an interpretation of Burton's psychology, which has been matured and dramatically realized in the poet's mind. Far from making prosaic direct borrowings as he did in *The Lovers Melancholy* and *The Fancies*, he does not even describe his melancholic before his appearance as he did in these plays and in *The Broken Heart* and *Loves Sacrifice*. Instead, Giovanni appears at once and step by

[18] Bullen, II, ii, n. 10.

step reveals his character in action. Ford even allows Giovanni's father and sister to make erroneous diagnoses, so confident is he that symptoms alone will make the melancholy clear. In the first act the Friar (who is no Burtonian) states the prognosis and suggests a treatment, which Giovanni tries. Thereafter, through four acts his melancholy drives him unimpeded to the catastrophe.

Perkin Warbeck cuts loose from the direct influence of Burton altogether, although there is no doubt that Ford's study of the treatise and frequent use of it, now over a period of years, rendered the history of the misguided pretender a congenial subject. Whereas the play stands apart from other Ford plays in its surprising grasp of political ideas and worthily fills one gap which Shakespeare left in his sequence of histories, Warbeck's delusion gives it a family resemblance to all Ford's work. At the outset the delusion is clearly stated, but there is no scientific analysis of it beyond the chance inference that it was caused by Margaret's sorcery. Nor is the body of the play largely taken up with its treatment as are all the plays before this. No friend undertakes to disillusion Warbeck, for no friend believes that he is afflicted. But every moment he is on the stage he exhibits his symptoms—if such they can be called when his delusion is complete and he is happy in it—acting his rôle even to the satisfaction of his enemies. Only at the end (Act V, Scene ii following), when the madman is helpless in the power of the English, do the familiar analytical speeches come: we are told what caused his delusion, how it developed and was confirmed; and one character furnishes us with the prognosis: hopeless.

The tragi-comedy *The Queen*, while similar in theme and in some aspects in technique to the first tragi-comedy, *The Lovers Melancholy*, clearly falls in point of time with the group of tragedies where Burton's influence is represented by a firmer grasp of the whole theme of mental aberration. There are few verbal echoes, no masque of madmen, no mediaeval physiology, though there is a case history. Ford does not use the long initial analysis, which he abandoned after *Loves Sacrifice*. Instead, Alphonso begins at once to show his symptoms, Pynto gives an early suggestion of the cause (which Sherman did not observe[19] and so quarrelled with what he considered Ford's failure to motivate Alphonso's misogyny, insurrection, and later jealousy), and we are soon thoroughly acquainted with his melancholy. Muretto takes Alphonso in charge in Act II, Scene ii. The body of the play is, like *The Lovers Melancholy*, preoccupied with demonstrating his treatment. But in *The Queen* it is a planned regimen with successive stages, in which Alphonso's symptoms increase in violence as it takes deeper and deeper effect. Then in the last act, rather than in the first, Muretto gives a concise diagnosis of what was the king's ailment, with symptoms, method of treatment, and prognosis. Introduced at the end it is less mechanical, for it has a dramatic function beyond exposition: its revelations are the final step in the treatment and are successful in bringing about the cure.

In *The Ladies Triall*, Ford's last known play, one incidental character is an off-hand sketch of the love-melancholic. There is no initial description of his affliction, no direct statement of the cause, and little demonstration of symptoms, for he appears only three times in the course of the whole play. But, although the character is drawn with a minimum of detail, it is notable for its clarity and for a certain warmth: Malfato is more human than many of his predecessors in melancholy. But even without Malfato *The Ladies Triall* would be a significant member of Ford's series of studies of the effect of melancholy. Its main plot presents a return to the situation dramatized in *The Broken Heart* and *Loves Sacrifice* with an all-important difference: Auria is jealous, but, whereas the other jealous heroes are melancholy (complete with causes, symptoms, diagnosis, treatment, prognosis, and—in Bassanes's case—cure), Auria is drawn with scrupulous care to avoid even the suggestion of melancholy. The play evidently means to ask "What will be the effect of a reasonable rather than a distempered jealousy?" and to answer "Since the jealousy is reasonable, the suspicion can be cleared up; hence the outcome will be happy."

[19] Sherman, "A New Play by John Ford," *Modern Language Notes*, XXIII (1908), 247-8.

THE EFFECT UPON CHARACTERS

The structural significance of melancholy in Ford's plays is very great. It controls the classification of characters in a play, for it draws into the ranks of serious characters those which had conventionally been considered more suitable for comedy. This is especially true of the eunuch, the cuckold, and the misogynist. Ford challenged the tradition of all these types. How differently the eunuch Octavio could have been handled can be seen within the play *The Fancies* in the character Spadone. Spadone is a supposed eunuch, a "gelded hobet-a-hoy,"[20] a "great male-baby,"[21] whose name is the Latin word for *eunuch,* used by Horace, Livy, and Juvenal. He is a member of the superlatively gross comic crew, the other members of which are: Nitido, the marquis's page who is yet a child, who has not "come to the honour of a beard yet,"[22] but hopes "to live to be a man";[23] Secco, the marquis's barber, not an old man as Sherman thought he was,[24] but eighteen years of age;[25] and Morosa, "the lady guardianess, the mother of the Fancies,"[26] sixty years old[27] (which is to say, very old, in Ford's time) and a bawd, "your old temptation, your she-devil."[28] The principal business of this noble crew is taunting each other on their sexual shortcomings, irregularities, or excesses. In their opening scene (I, ii) Spadone is ridiculed by Secco:

Sirrah Spadone, I will make thee a man; a man, dost hear? I say, a man;[29]

and by Nitido, singing

And still the urchin would, but could not do.[30]

Spadone answers in kind and swears revenge. The marriage of Secco and Morosa takes place. At the dance attending the wedding ceremony (II, ii), it occurs to Spadone that he can be

[20] *The Fancies,* IV, i (Bullen, II, 293). Grose defines *hobberdehoy:* "half a man and half a boy; a lad between both."
[21] *The Fancies,* V, ii (Bullen, II, 310).
[22] *ibid.,* III, iii (Bullen, II, 275).   [23] *ibid.,* IV, i (Bullen, II, 292).
[24] *Ford's Debt.*   [25] *The Fancies,* I, ii (Bullen, II, 233, 235).
[26] *ibid.* (Bullen, II, 235).   [27] *ibid.* See also IV, i (Bullen, II, 294).
[28] *ibid.,* III, iii (Bullen, II, 283).   [29] Bullen, II, 234.
[30] Bullen, II, 237.

revenged on his two tormentors by reporting to Secco that
Nitido has cuckolded him. He does so at the first opportunity
(III, iii), and Secco publicly disgraces his bride by pinching
her and calling her "most filthy names."[31] This leads to two
coarse farcical scenes. In one (IV, i) Secco forces the supposedly offending page, choking with a halter around his throat,
to take down his breeches, ready to be whipped. At the last
minute Spadone acts the simpleton and pretends ignorance of
the whole business. Spadone's desire for revenge is satisfied
with thus bringing Nitido within sight of the lash and by
publicly making a suspicious fool of Secco. In the other scene
(V, ii) Secco takes revengé on Spadone for his hoax by holding him helpless in his barber chair, his face and eyes covered
with a stinking mud-paste, while he threatens to cut his throat.
All now seem to feel that they have gotten even with each other,
and they make it up: "We forget what hath passed, and are
fellows and friends again."[32] Through all this there is a constant stream of obscene innuendo at the expense of one or other
of the characters. What the supposed eunuch has to endure is
such jibes as

> What a terrible sight to a libbed breech is a sow-gelder;[33]

> . . . the nymphs need not fear the evidence of thy mortal-
> ity:—go, put on a clean bib, and spin amongst the nuns, sing
> 'em a bawdy song: all the children thou gettest shall be chris-
> tened in wassail-bowls, and turned into a college of men-
> midwives;[34]

while he is not beyond making sport of himself, thus:

> Twit me with the decrement of my pendants! though I am
> made a gelding, and, like a tame buck, have lost my dowsets,
> . . . yet I scorn to be jeered by any checker-approved bar-
> barian of ye all;[35]

and willingly consents to dance at Secco's wedding, for he is
"not the heaviest in the company."[36] Whether this plot and

[31] Bullen, II, 279.   [32] Bullen, II, 315.
[33] *The Fancies*, I, ii (Bullen, II, 236).   [34] *ibid*. (Bullen, II, 237).
[35] *ibid*. (Bullen, II, 234).   [36] *ibid*., II, ii (Bullen, II, 259).

these remarks be funny I shall not argue; but they offer the strongest contrast to the restraint and dignity with which Octavio's affliction is handled by the serious characters.

The old-man-husband, jealous of his wife and fearful of horns, is also rendered serious by melancholy. While it is true that cuckoldry, one of the most current themes in Elizabethan drama, is equally serviceable as tragedy and comedy, seldom have the two uses been combined in a single character as in Bassanes. Though he is at the very heart of the tragic plot, the rant and lewdness of his speeches and actions in Act II, Scene i, taken in conjunction with the confidential remarks aside (e.g. "*Phulas* Here's a sweet life!")[37] indicate that his function is partly comic. The likelihood of this interpretation is increased by the fact that there is no comic crew in *The Broken Heart* as there is in every other extant Ford play. Bassanes's equivocal position between absurd and pathetic strongly recalls a similar old man, Meleander, whose melancholy also is violent and noisy. Now since *The Lovers Melancholy* and *The Broken Heart* were acted by the King's Company, the very disparity of the traits combined in Meleander and Bassanes suggests that Ford wrote the part with the peculiar talents of a particular actor in mind. At all events, it is the treatment of each character's melancholy that restores him to the serious ranks, just as it is the symptoms of his melancholy that make him the butt of the laughter of the vulgar.

The misogynist, Alphonso, is rendered serious by melancholy. Misogyny, as the principal theme of a play, is not of frequent occurrence in Elizabethan drama, though as an incidental idea it is practically universal. There is one play, however, Beaumont and Fletcher's *The Woman-Hater*, which shows how differently Alphonso might have been handled in comedy. Oriana, the beautiful lady of the play, is driven by a sudden storm to take refuge in the house of the known misogynist, Gondarino. She uses the opportunity to torment him with amorous advances, which it is beyond his power either to counter or to enjoy. A little later the same storm brings the Duke, who is in

[37] *The Broken Heart,* II, i (Sherman, p. 164).

love with Oriana, to Gondarino's house. There follows a double misunderstanding: Gondarino concludes that Oriana is unchaste and that he is being made a pander to the Duke's amours; while the Duke believes that Gondarino's misogyny is only a mask for his lust, and therefore doubts Oriana's chastity. It is not before Oriana has suffered the indignity of being sent by Gondarino to live in a house of ill repute that her character is cleared and the Duke takes her as his wife.

Gondarino is one of a group of "humorous" types, presented, in the manner of Jonson or Marston, for their satirical effect: Lazarello, the glutton; Mercer, the gullible citizen-merchant; Lucio, the upstart fop-courtier; and the court intelligencer.[38] A typical scene presenting Gondarino's ruling passion is that (V, ii) in which he is tied to a chair in order that he may be helpless to ward off the amorous dalliance of a troop of ladies who kiss him, sit on his knees, stroke his hair, and try to warm his cold hands, until he cries out:

> I pronounce perdition to ye all; ye are a parcel of that damned crew that fell down with *Lucifer,* and here ye staid on earth to plague poor men.[39]

Alphonso's humour is exactly the same as this, but he is presented with great soberness. His melancholy and its implications make his misogyny serious business.

THE EFFECT UPON ACTION

The structural significance of melancholy in the action of a play is as great as it is in determination of the characters. Melancholy poses the dramatic problem, determines the selection of scenes, motivates the character's acts, and specifies the denouement.

In *The Lovers Melancholy* Agenor's wickedness set the whole sequence of events in motion. Still his influence is no more, for he is dead before the opening of the play. The melancholy which is the result of his misdeeds is the motive

---

[38] An intelligencer is one who brings informations, "pick'd out of broken words, in mens common talk, which, with his malicious mis-application, he hopes will seem dangerous." *The Woman-Hater,* I, iii (Waller, X, 81).
[39] *ibid.,* V, ii (Waller, X, 140).

power of the play itself. Melancholy is destroying the prince's
character, rendering him incapable of attending to business,
preventing his marrying, disappointing the hope of his dynasty,
making the courtiers fretful, the people rebellious, and the
neighboring nations dangerous. Melancholy is killing old
Meleander, breaking Cleophila's heart, and destroying the hope
of their family also by standing in the way of her marriage
with Amethus. These far-reaching results bring the play into
sharp contrast with the mere melancholy in disposition of Thirsis and Silvia in Daniel's play, *Hymen's Triumph*, 1615, which
Sherman suggested[40] as a source for *The Lovers Melancholy*.
Thirsis is not anything beyond the typical grief-stricken lover
of the pastoral tradition. He "afflicts himselfe in solitarinesse,"[41]
avoiding light and company[42] and seeing nobody but his best
friend to whom he confides his sadness for "you were reseru'd
To tell me she was lost."[43] Ford's addition of true melancholy
extended the interest from a pastoral shepherd's sorrow to the
fateful results of that sorrow. But a play must have events as
well as emotionalism. What the passive melancholy of Palador
and Meleander could not furnish was supplied from the outside,
by the agencies which combined to cure their ailment. Melancholy, then, causes all the action of the play as well.

In *The Fancies* Octavio's melancholy is the unifying and
motivating force of the play. Without Octavio the absurd
Bower of Fancies could not be, without his melancholy jealousy
the secret of the Bower could not be preserved, without both
of these there could be no play. Palador's passive melancholy
brought about only a plan for the cure of that affliction, but
Octavio's seemingly immoral advances occasion the misunder-
standings, quarrels, rejected suits, and threatened duel which
are the main business of the play. In *The Broken Heart* Bassanes's jealousy is the basis of Penthea's suffering, melancholy,
madness, and suicide, and the occasion for Orgilus's disguise.
Even after Bassanes has served this far-reaching structural
purpose, his dramatic life is continued and a new interest is

[40] *Ford's Debt.*
[41] *Hymen's Triumph*, III, i (Grosart, III, 368).
[42] *ibid.*, III, ii (Grosart, III, 370).   [43] *ibid.*, I, i (Grosart, III, 340).

created in the character for himself by an ingenious development of his melancholy, which is supported by the authority of Burton : Bassanes undertakes his own cure, by patience, and succeeds. Ithocles's melancholy provides the groundwork for the whole situation in that it caused the brutal forced marriage of Penthea. Together the melancholies motivate Orgilus's murder of Ithocles, which in turn causes the death of Calantha.

The way Philippo's two melancholies in *Loves Sacrifice* are treated is what makes the difference between this play and *The Broken Heart* and furnishes the refutation to Richard Crashaw's clever epigram

> Thou cheat'st us, Ford ; mak'st one seem two by art :
> What is Love's Sacrifice but the Broken Heart ?[44]

His plain melancholy, being uncured, together with the circumstances of his old age and Bianca's birth, fortune, and behaviour, is the irresistible cause of his jealous melancholy. His jealous melancholy motivates the murder of Bianca, which in turn occasions Fernando's and Philippo's suicides. The fact that Philippo's condition is thus fully accounted for renders his violence more legitimate, and less perversely brutal than Bassanes's, and makes the whole action more credible than that of *The Broken Heart*. Since Philippo's jealous melancholy does not attain the cure that Bassanes's does, the aggrieved husband and the avenger can be joined in one person, the storm is concentrated, and the brutality of the catastrophe thus further justified. Philippo is much less the "well-meaning dotard" than is Bassanes, and Ford has laid a firmer psychological groundwork than that of *The Broken Heart* rather than "lost his way through a great part of this drama."

In *'Tis Pitty* the importance of melancholy to the action is almost too clear to justify stating it. Giovanni's melancholy is the sole cause of, and the only irrefutable excuse for, his yielding to his passion, which in turn brings Annabella, Florio, Soranzo, and Giovanni himself down to disgrace and death. Mr. T. S. Eliot seeks the justification of the revolutionary thesis of *'Tis Pitty* in the traditional concept of a love so com-

---

[44] Bullen, I, lxxix.

manding as to warrant any breach of convention. But this love
he cannot find in the play:

> . . . the passion of Giovanni and Annabella is not shown as an
> affinity of temperament due to identity of blood; it hardly rises
> above the purely carnal infatuation. In *Antony and Cleopatra*
> (which is no more an apology for adultery than *'Tis Pity*
> is an apology for incest) we are made to feel convinced of an
> overpowering attraction towards each other of two per-
> sons, not only in defiance of conventional morality, but against
> self-interest. . . . But Giovanni is merely selfish and self-
> willed, of a temperament to want a thing the more because it is
> forbidden; Annabella is pliant, vacillating and negative: the
> one almost a monster of egotism, the other virtually a moral
> defective. . . . In short, the play has not the general significance
> and emotional depth (for the two go together) without which
> no such action can be justified; and this defect separates it
> completely from the best plays of Webster, Middleton and
> Tourneur.[45]

By giving Giovanni an irresistible motivation, melancholy supplies an alternative justification for the thesis of the play and
renders Eliot's objection invalid.

In *Perkin Warbeck* Warbeck's delusion is the whole play in
a sense not true elsewhere except as Palador's and Meleander's
was the whole of *The Lovers Melancholy*. And it causes not
only the death of the hero (who could not accept proffered forgiveness, for he was incapable of relinquishing his delusion)
but the disaster of his wife and with her of the Gordon family,
and involves two kings and the title to a throne, nobles, diplo-
mats, armies, battles, needless deaths and the domestic and
foreign affairs of two nations. In *The Queen,* as in *The Lovers
Melancholy*, the melancholy produces an intense conflict of
emotions but no action. Everything is negative: Alphonso will
not see the Queen and will not attend to affairs of state. It is
the treatment which is the play and produces the events: the
contrary emotions of love and jealousy which Muretto succeeds
in arousing in Philippo place the Queen's life in jeopardy on
a charge of adultery and Petruchi's on a charge of treason,

[45] T. S. Eliot, *Selected Essays,* 1917-1932 (New York: Harcourt, Brace
and Company), pp. 174-5.

and initiate the trial by combat. When the cure is effected, the conflict of emotions is supplanted by mutual respect and love, the threatening action is dissolved, and the commonwealth is restored to peace and security under the government of united monarchs. Stuart Sherman said[46] of *The Queen* that the germinal idea of the play was the same as that of *The Lovers Melancholy*: "The King is the patient, Muretto is the doctor, the Queen is the cure." While enforcing the general similarity of the plays, I have perhaps shown how unjustly summary this comment is. Palador and Meleander are suffering from melancholy caused by the loss of Eroclea, and the cure is simply her return. All the ministrations of the Burtonian physician go for nought, and he is the laughingstock of the play. But in *The Queen*, the Queen is always present; her presence makes the king's ailment go steadily from bad to worse. Muretto treats him by the exact administration of a Burtonian principle, is successful, and receives the thankful commendation of all. The psychological pattern is a much more complex one in *The Queen*, and the melancholic is shown in a way evidently beyond the power of the dramatist in 1628—namely, in the process of growth.

CONTRAST WITH TOURNEUR AND WEBSTER

The controlling force that melancholy has in the action of Ford's plays sets him off from all his contemporaries, even his closest affinities, Tourneur and Webster. In many a sensational scene Tourneur's characters commit atrocities which can only be explained as sheer diabolism; in similar scenes in Ford, the characters' actions are explained as the recognized prognostics of their diseases. Thus Ford escapes the charge of being melodramatic at the same time that he satisfies his audience's taste for strong meat. Webster is a closer parallel. He reveals the same analytical comprehension of the subject that Ford does. In *The Duchess of Malfi* we find four people whom other characters call melancholy: the Duchess, Bosola, the Cardinal, and the Duke. In how many of these cases is the word used in a free, romantic sense—"melancholy in disposition, improperly

---

[46] In the article referred to above, n. 19, p. 248.

so called"? I believe in two: the Duchess and the Cardinal. Just
before the strangulation of the Duchess, the Duke speaks of his
sister's melancholy: he is curious to know what gives her her
unaccountable calmness:

> Her mellancholly seemes to be fortifide
> With a strange disdaine.[47]

But all through the spectacular horrors (dead-man's hand, wax
images of Antonio and their children dead) which the Duke
sets out to torture her mind, and in spite of the howling of a
troop of madmen, she remains in complete self-control. It may
be she "speaks the dialect of despair,"[48] yet if there be anything
notable about her action in this extraordinary scene, it is that
she holds calmly to the right line of reason in a world
where everything seems to have gone mad, rather than that she
gives way. The Cardinal, we are told, "is growne wondrous
mellancholly"[49] since the execution of the Duchess. This also is
"melancholy in disposition" only. The Cardinal, having ordered
that the Duchess be strangled, and having successfully shifted
the blame for the order to the Duke, is fearful lest the secret
be discovered. Fear is a cause of melancholy, but only unreasoned fear, not the natural dread that a criminal feels when
discovery is imminent.

Bosola, and to a greater degree the Duke, however, are suffering from true melancholy. Bosola presents an interesting case
of the developing melancholic. Until the time of his connivance
at the murder of the Duchess, his melancholy has been em-
phatically that of the malcontent—seven years of slavery in the
galleys as punishment for a "notorious murther," which " 'twas
thought The Cardinall suborn'd,"[50] have taught him to look for
sustenance to the employ of evil princes in desperate enterprises.
He has assumed for the purpose the mask of cynicism about

---

[47] *Duchess of Malfi*, IV, i (Lucas, II, 89).
[48] Lamb (Lucas, IV, 179, n. 4).
[49] *Duchess of Malfi*, V, ii (Lucas, II, 111).
[50] *ibid.*, I, i (Lucas, II, 38-9).

women and "the world" which is the conventional pose of the
Elizabethan villain. The Duke understands it as such:

> Be your selfe:
> Keepe your old garbe of melencholly: 'twill expresse
> You envy those that stand above your reach,
> Yet strive not to come neere'em: This will gaine
> Accesse, to private lodgings, where your selfe
> May (like a pollitique dormouse—[51]

And the Cardinal mistakes Bosola's true melancholy later as the
same thing, much to his own disadvantage:

> *Card.* I have honors in store for thee.
> *Bos.* There are a many wayes that conduct to seeming
> Honor, and some of them very durty ones.
> *Card.* Throw to the divell
> Thy mellancholly—the fire burnes well,
> What neede we keepe a-stirring of't, and make
> A greater smoother? thou wilt kill *Antonio*?[52]

The Cardinal's words mean, in effect, "use your disguise of
malcontentism when advantageous, but not now; it is only a
hindrance in the present business." In the interim true melancholy has overtaken Bosola. Real pity and remorse strike him
for the first time as he stares at the dead body of the Duchess,
with his soul suffering in a "sencible Hell": "that we cannot
be suffer'd To doe good when we have a mind to it!"[53] This
feeling rapidly grows beyond his control (the Cardinal notices
a wild and ghastly look on his face),[54] and torments him with
hallucinations: "Still me thinkes the Dutchesse Haunts me:
there, there!—'tis nothing but my mellancholy."[55] His heart
really breaks at the bungling murder of Antonio,[56] and he dies
with a sense of complete despair in a wasted life:

---

[51] *ibid.* (Lucas, II, 44-5).   [52] *ibid.,* V, ii (Lucas, I., 115).
[53] *ibid.,* IV, ii (Lucas, II, 103).
[54] *ibid.,* V, ii (Lucas, II, 109); V, v (Lucas, II, 121).
[55] *ibid.,* V, ii (Lucas, II, 116).
[56] *ibid.,* V, iv (Lucas, II, 120):
     "Breake heart!"
     It is possible, of course, that this speech is addressed to Antonio rather
than to himself.

Yes, I hold my weary soule in my teeth,
.   .   .   .   my selfe,
(That was an Actor in the maine of all,
Much 'gainst mine owne good nature, yet i' th' end
Neglected).[57]

There is none of the duality of the malcontent in this valedictory Bosola. The Duke's case is too clear to require demonstration. Weaker in evil purposes than his villain instrument, he is overcome at once with fear and remorse at the death of the Duchess and has passed through melancholy and gone completely mad before we see him again. The doctor's diagnosis of his disease in Act V, Scene ii as lycanthropia and his description of it are, in all probability, directly from the pages of Burton.

But while there may be true melancholy in Webster's play, it is not used as the motivating force of the play. Melancholy is one of the results of a criminal act, not the cause of crime as in Ford; the incidental evidence of a character's disintegration, not the basic unifying element in his personality. In Webster the character is still the villain; in Ford melancholy itself has taken over.

THE EFFECT UPON THOUGHT

Melancholy revolutionizes the thought of a play. It is the principle of confusion: it upsets all the laws, mental, moral, and social of the world into which it enters. It picks its victim with no logic perceptible to him and pursues him like a Fate which he is equally powerless to avoid, to counter, or to control. It destroys his self-mastery in thought and action, and leads him to violate the conventions of moral behaviour. His fellow-mortals are aghast, but, realizing what has happened, undertake to help him, until that time when they too may catch something of the contagion. Then the whole little world of the play is in turmoil. The result of this abdication of reason is inevitably disaster. Octavio, Romanello, and Malfato pay for their intellectual misfortune with continued unhappiness; Ithocles, Penthea, Orgilus, Giovanni, Philippo, and Warbeck, with death. Contrariwise the reward for reenthronement of reason is hap-

[57] *ibid.*, V, v (Lucas, II, 123).

piness after great distress. Because Palador, Meleander, Bassanes, and Alphonso rewin their equilibrium, they rewin with it their peace and honourable places in the world. Adurni, whose mind is not distempered, can deliver his suspicion over to logic and judgment and show all the other characters the way to happiness.

This effect of melancholy serves to illuminate one of the most difficult phases of the study of Ford: his philosophy and morality. He has been traditionally accused of confusion of moral values or even of wilful equivocation. But one now sees that this charge is due in part to the common fallacy of identifying the characters' thoughts with those of the playwright. The characters' moral thinking is obviously confused—it was deranged by melancholy. But Ford's is not necessarily so. When one looks at the justice being meted out in the fifth act, one sees that the premium is not only upon probity of action but upon clarity of mind: straight-thinking is still a virtue (indeed it is the greatest virtue) and obliquity still brings its own punishment. Ford has traditionally been disparaged as the purveyor of emotionalism. One now observes that he is much more the intellectualist than he has been given credit for: he is vitally interested in the study of the mind, its function and malfunction, and in the personal, social, and political results of malfunction. The playwright must still bear the burden, however, of what blame attaches to him for being too much interested in oblique subjects and for dissolving their sin in a cup of sweetness[58] by treating them with sympathy and clothing them in great poetry.

THE EFFECT UPON SYMPATHY

Melancholy increases the pathos of a play. In direct proportion as the poet succeeds in making the reader credit melancholy with sovereign power over the events and thought of the play. the characters win the sympathy and pity which we always accord the helpless victim. Sometimes it is not much. For example, instead of being sorry for Octavio, the reader is apt merely not to blame him, and to be glad when he can end his

[58] Ward, *A History of English Dramatic Literature*, III, 78.

perusal of the play and be free from its repellant company. But if it were not for Octavio's melancholy, the reader would certainly be actively disgusted with his senile amorousness. Nor can the reader be particularly sorry for Alphonso. Yet his melancholy saves Alphonso from contempt for gross ingratitude. Sympathy for Warbeck is much greater. Whatever he may have done in the past, in the time of the play his delusion renders him pitiable. At no time is he more kingly or pathetic than when, in his extreme hour, the consistency of his delusion makes him unable to humble his pride and save his neck as Simnel does by renouncing his claims. Without his delusion Warbeck would have been a fool.

In the great plays melancholy is the very principle of tragedy itself. It is the character's tragic flaw, which imbues all his wickedness and violence in the colours of martyrdom. Philippo's initial melancholy is a sort of fate for him, which predestined his jealous melancholy. Thereafter he has only a sorrowful choice: if Bianca lives, he is tortured with suspicion; if she dies, he is grief-stricken and can expiate his violence only with suicide. Giovanni's melancholy also is the fate which drives him on the rocks. He is the philosopher among the melancholy characters, for he realizes that he must establish a "Rule of Nature" if he is to relieve his own shoulders of the awful responsibility for his actions. Therefore he strives by constant repetition to make the Friar (and the reader) accept this idea. But he does not go so far as to perceive that this very Rule of Nature *is* his atheistic melancholy. Even if he had done so, labelling his Fate would not have saved him from its consequences. The pathetic effect of melancholy is greatest, perhaps, in *The Broken Heart*. We may be repelled from sympathy with Bassanes by the gross outrage of his scenes with Penthea, but we are won to sympathy by his self-cure. Ford is the poet of repressed emotion, of silent suffering. "There is coldness and restraint in much of his work; a grave and chill dignity in which the emotions seem to be recollected rather than felt; recollected not merely in tranquillity, but in spellbound stillness."[59] In *The Broken Heart* this mood receives its most various and effective

[59] Ellis-Fermor, p. 229.

illustration: Ithocles meets his murderer with a calm resolution
not to whine, shrink, or beg compassion; Orgilus refuses to
show any distress as ice which no heat can ever thaw comes
to sit about his heart; and Calantha but danced the more
gaily

> When one newes straight came hudling on another
> Of death, and death, and death.[60]

It is as a peer to this group of broken hearts that Bassanes takes
his place in the last two acts of the play. The patience which is
to cure his jealousy (too late to forestall the tragic climax) is
also the signal of his deep remorse: he not only silently endures
the hurt of seeing Penthea mad,

> What a foole am I
> To bandy passion! E're I'le speake a word,
> I will looke on and burst,[61]

but encourages Orgilus and Ithocles to prod the wound by
keeping them in ignorance of his reformation. Orgilus seals
Bassanes's admission to the broken hearts a little later by
forgiving him and thereafter treating him as a brother by
right of common sorrow, both in his tragic secret (the death
of Penthea) and in the closing pageantry of the play. Without
their melancholy Philippo, Giovanni, and Bassanes would have
been inhuman, their actions monstrous.

THE SOURCE OF FORD'S INTEREST

It is not possible at this distance and with the fragmentary
biographical records which have come down to us to arrive at an
explanation of Ford's absorbing interest in the subject of melancholy. As a member of a group notable for its social activity
and intellectual vitality—the Templars—he was of course im-

---

[60] *The Broken Heart,* V, iii (Sherman, p. 267).

[61] *ibid.,* IV, ii (Sherman, p. 232). My interpretation depends upon the ac-
ceptance of Dyce's emendation of "bandy" for "bawdy" of the Quarto. In
three similar passages, *The Lovers Melancholy,* V, i (Bullen, I, 102), *The
Fancies,* V, i (Bullen, II, 303), and V, iii (Bullen, II, 315), "bandy" has the
support of the Quarto, and I have not found "bawdy" used in this construction. Besides Bassanes has not been a "fool to bawdy passion," whereas he
has been foolishly bandying passion in speeches with Orgilus.

mersed in the ideas current in his time, and melancholy was an important one of these. In explanation of the general interest in melancholy in disposition in the seventeenth century Knight[62] suggests three facts: a growing interest in psychology; a new realization of the imminence of death, impressed by the Plagues; the changed economic and social organization of the seventeenth century, and the consequent thwarting of ambition in young men who found no scope for their talents. All of these apply to Ford—the first two obviously, for he was a product of the time. And what is known of his life would seem to indicate that he was thwarted. Although he was trained in the law and probably resided all his life at the Temple,[63] no record of any legal business in which he took part has ever been found. Idleness and discontent is implied in his childish rebellion against the necessary discipline of the Temple, not only in youth but in full maturity.[64] The late age (thirty-five) at which he began to give most of his energies to the drama suggests two long decades (entrance into the Temple, 1602, to *The Witch of Edmonton*, 1621) during which he struggled to find his place in the world. There is frustration in the sulky and contemptuous air he affects in many of his Dedications. He wants it understood, in *The Lovers Melancholy,* for example, that he is only a gentleman idly exercising one of his talents; he does not care to please the many; nobody can reproach him with having printed a play before, and it is very possible that he will not do so again.[65]

Another possible explanation of Ford's interest in the subject of melancholy should be suggested. Burton undertook his study for the avowed purpose of curing an "imposthume" in his own head. Besides, he says, one must needs scratch where it itches.[66] On the other hand he gave solemn warning more than once[67] that the subject had better be let alone. Young physicians often appropriate to themselves the symptoms of the diseases they

[62] *Drama & Society,* pp. 315 ff.
[63] Sargeaunt, "John Ford at the Middle Temple," *The Review of English Studies,* VIII (1932), 69-71.
[64] *ibid.*   [65] See above, p. 30.
[66] Burton, I, 18.   [67] *ibid.,* I, 38, 446.

study, and thus become ill. It is worth the guess—and it is only a guess, for there is no evidence beyond the plays themselves—either that because he read Burton, Ford himself became afflicted with true melancholy, or that being so afflicted, he turned to the study of Burton for help and solace. In any case he found in the *Anatomy* a rich vein, which he worked long and profitably.

BIBLIOGRAPHY

This bibliography includes titles of 1) books and articles referred to by short title in the notes, 2) other books of interest to the student of Ford.

M.A. "The Phoenix Society—'Tis Pitty Shees a Whore,' " *The Spectator* (London), CXXX (1923), 184-5.

Adams, J. Q. *The Dramatic Records of Sir Henry Herbert, Master of the Revels, 1623-1673.* (Cornell Studies in English, III.) New Haven, 1917.

————— *Shakespearean Playhouses.* Boston, 1917.

Anderson, R. L. *Elizabethan Psychology and Shakespeare's Plays.* (University of Iowa, Humanistic Studies, Vol. III, No. 4.) Iowa City, Iowa, 1927.

Arber, Edward, Ed. *A Transcript of the Registers of the Company of Stationers of London; 1554-1640 A.D.* Birmingham, 1875-1894.

Babb, Lawrence. "Abnormal Psychology in John Ford's *Perkin Warbeck*," *Modern Language Notes,* LI (1936), 234-7.

Beaumont, Francis and Fletcher, John. *The Works of Francis Beaumont and John Fletcher.* Ed. Arnold Glover and A. R. Waller. Cambridge, 1905-1912.

Bieber, G. A. *Der Melancholikertypus Shakespeares und sein Ursprung.* (Anglistische Arbeiten, hrsg. von L. L. Schücking, III.) Heidelberg, 1913.

Bradbrook, M. C. "John Ford," *Themes and Conventions of Elizabethan Tragedy.* Cambridge, 1935.

Bullen, A. H. Article, "Robert Burton," *Dictionary of National Biography.*

————— Article, "John Ford," *Dictionary of National Biography.*

————— Ed. *The Works of John Ford.* London, 1895.

Burton, Robert. *The Anatomy of Melancholy.* Ed. Floyd Dell and Paul Jordan-Smith. New York, 1927.

————— *The Anatomy of Melancholy.* Ed. A. R. Shilleto. London, 1893.

Choyce Drollery, Songs & Sonnets; Being a Collection of Divers Excellent Pieces of Poetry of Several Eminent Authors, 1656. Ed. J. Woodfall Ebsworth. Boston, Lincolnshire, 1876.

Cochnower, M. E. "John Ford," *Seventeenth Century Studies.* Ed. Robert Shafer. Princeton University Press for the University of Cincinnati, 1933.

Cockeram, Henry. *The English Dictionarie of 1623.* Ed. C. B. Tinker. New York, 1930.

Courthope, W. J. "The Last Days of the Poetic Drama: Massinger and Ford," *A History of English Poetry.* New York, 1903.

Creizenach, W. M. A. *The English Drama in the Age of Shakespeare.* Philadelphia, 1916.

Daniel, Samuel. *The Complete Works in Verse and Prose.* Ed. A. B. Grosart. London, 1885-1896.

du Tillet, Jacques. "Représentation de l'Œuvre: *Annabella,* drame en cinq actes, de John Ford, traduction de M. Maurice Maeterlinck," *Revue Bleue (Revue Politique et Littéraire),* Ser. IV, Vol. II, No. 20 (1894), 633-6.

Eliot, T. S. "John Ford," *Selected Essays, 1917-1932.* New York, 1932.

Ellis-Fermor, U. M. *The Jacobean Drama.* London, 1936.

Fleay, F. G. *A Biographical Chronicle of the English Drama, 1559-1642.* London, 1891.

Ford, John. Commendatory Verse to Brome *The Northern Lass.* In Brome, *Dramatic Works,* III, xi. London, 1873.

────── Commendatory Verse to Massinger *The Great Duke of Florence.* In edition of J. M. Stochholm, p. 6. Baltimore, 1933.

────── Commendatory Verse to Massinger *The Roman Actor.* In edition of W. L. Sandidge, p. 49. Princeton, 1929.

────── Commendatory Verse to Webster *The Duchess of Malfi.* In edition of F. L. Lucas, II, 35. London, 1927.

────── *A Critical Edition of Ford's Perkin Warbeck.* Ed. M. C. Struble. (University of Washington Publications in Language and Literature, III.) Seattle, 1926.

────── *The Queen, or The Excellency of Her Sex.* Ed. W. Bang. (Materialien zur Kunde des älteren Englischen Dramas, XIII. 1906.)

────── *'Tis Pity She's a Whore* and *The Broken Heart.* Ed. S. P. Sherman. (Belles Lettres Series.) Boston, 1915.

────── *The Dramatic Works of John Ford.* With an introduction and explanatory notes by Henry Weber. Edinburgh, 1811.

Bibliography 119

Ford, John. *The Dramatic Works of John Ford*. With notes critical and explanatory by W. Gifford, Esq. London, 1827.

———— *The Dramatic Works of Massinger and Ford*. With an introduction by Hartley Coleridge. London, 1839.

———— *The Works of John Ford*. With notes critical and explanatory by William Gifford, Esq. A new edition, carefully revised, with additions to the text and to the notes by the Rev. Alexander Dyce. London, 1869.

———— *The Works of John Ford*. Edited by William Gifford with additions by Rev. Alexander Dyce. Now reissued with further additions [by A. H. Bullen]. London, 1895.

———— *John Fordes dramatische Werke*. In Neudruck herausgegeben von W. Bang. Erster Band. (Materialien zur Kunde des älteren Englischen Dramas, XXIII). Louvain, 1908. (Contains S. P. Sherman's essay, "Forde's Contribution to the Decadence of the Drama," *The Lovers Melancholy*, and *Loves Sacrifice*.)

———— *John Ford's Dramatic Works*. Reprinted from the original quartos. Ed. Henry de Vocht. (Materials for the Study of the Old English Drama, New Series, I.) Louvain, 1927. (Contains *The Broken Heart, 'Tis Pitty Shee's a Whore, The Chronicle Historie of Perkin Warbeck, The Fancies, Chast and Noble*, and *The Ladies Triall*.)

Forsythe, R. S. *The Relations of Shirley's Plays to the Elizabethan Drama*. New York, 1914.

Freeburg, V. O. *Disguise Plots in Elizabethan Drama*. New York, 1915.

[Gifford, William] "*Ford's Dramatic Works*, by Weber," *The Quarterly Review*, VI (1811), 462-87. A review of Weber's edition.

Goodchild, Donald. *The Literature and Philosophy of Melancholy at the End of the Renaissance*. Princeton Dissertation, 1926. MS. in Princeton University Library.

Greg, W. W. *A List of Masques, Pageants, &c*. London, Feb. 1902.

Grose, Francis. *A Classical Dictionary of the Vulgar Tongue*. London, 1785.

E. H. "John Ford," *The Academy*, LX (1901), 429-30.

Hanford, J. H. *A Milton Handbook*. New York, 1936.

Hannemann, Eduard. *Metrische Untersuchungen zu John Ford*. Halle, 1888.

Hazlitt, William. *Lectures Chiefly on the Dramatic Literature of the Age of Elizabeth*. London, 1840.

120   Bibliography

Hunt, M. L. *Thomas Dekker; A Study.* New York, 1911.

[Jeffrey, Francis.] "Ford's *Dramatic Works,*" *The Edinburgh Review,* XVIII (1811), 275-304.

Jonson, Ben. *Plays.* Ed. Brinsley Nicholson and C. H. Herford. (The Mermaid Series.) New York [1893-1894].

Knights, L. C. *Drama & Society in the Age of Jonson.* London, 1937.

Koeppel, Emil. *Quellen-Studien zu den Dramen George Chapman's, Philip Massinger's und John Ford's.* Strassburg, 1897.

—— *Studien über Shakespeare's Wirkung auf zeitgenössische Dramatiker.* (Materialien zur Kunde des älteren Englischen Dramas, IX. 1905.)

—— *Studien zur Geschichte der Italienischen Novelle.* (Quellen und Forschungen zur Sprach- und Culturgeschichte, LXX.)

Lamb, Charles. *The Works of Charles and Mary Lamb.* Ed. E. V. Lucas. London, 1903 [-1905].

Lilly, William. *An Introduction to Astrology.* Ed. Zadkiel. London, 1835.

MacCarthy, Desmond. "Ford and the Phoenix," *New Statesman,* XX (1923), 514-15.

—— "The Poet of Satanism," *The Nation and the Athenaeum,* XXXII (1923), 698.

Marston, John. *The Works of John Marston.* Ed. A. H. Bullen. Boston, 1887.

Massinger, Philip. *The Unnatural Combat.* Ed. R. S. Telfer. (Princeton Studies in English, VII.) Princeton, 1932.

Milton, John. *The Student's Milton.* Ed. F. A. Patterson. New York, 1930.

Murray, J. T. *English Dramatic Companies, 1558-1642.* Boston, 1910.

Nason, A. H. *James Shirley, Dramatist.* New York, 1915.

Neilson, W. A. Article, "Ford and Shirley," *The Cambridge History of English Literature.*

Nungezer, Edwin. *A Dictionary of Actors and of Other Persons Associated with the Public Representation of Plays in England before 1642.* (Cornell Studies in English, XIII.) New Haven, 1929.

Oliphant, E. H. C. *The Plays of Beaumont and Fletcher.* New Haven, 1927.

O'Sullivan, M. I. "Hamlet and Dr. Timothy Bright," *Publications of the Modern Language Association,* XLI (1926), 667-79.

Parry, J. J. "A Seventeenth Century Gallery of Poets," *The Journal of English and Germanic Philology*, XIX (1920), 270-7.

Pierce, F. E. "The Sequence of Ford's Plays," *The Nation*, XCII (1911), 9-10.

Randolph, Thomas. *Poetical and Dramatic Works of Thomas Randolph*. Ed. W. Carew Hazlitt. London, 1875.

Reed, A. L. *The Background of Gray's Elegy; A Study in the Taste for Melancholy Poetry, 1700-1751*. New York, 1924.

Sargeaunt, M. Joan. *John Ford*. Oxford, 1935.

────── "John Ford at the Middle Temple," *The Review of English Studies*, VIII (1932), 69-71.

────── "Bequests to John Ford," *The Review of English Studies*, IX (1933), 447-8.

────── "Writings Ascribed to John Ford by Joseph Hunter in *Chorus Vatum*," *The Review of English Studies*, X (1934), 165-76.

Schelling, F. E. *Elizabethan Drama*, 1558-1642. Boston, 1908.

────── *Elizabethan Playwrights*. New York, 1925.

Sensabaugh, G. F. "Burton's Influence on Ford's *The Lover's Melancholy*," *Studies in Philology*, XXXIII (1936), 545-71.

────── "John Ford and Platonic Love in the Court," *Studies in Philology*, XXXVI (1939), 206-26.

Shakespeare, William. *Works*. Ed. W. J. Craig and Edward Dowden. (Oxford Edition.) Oxford, 1925-1927.

Shanks, Edward. "'Tis Pity She's a Whore," *Outlook* (London), LI (1923), 97.

Sherman, S. P. Ed. *'Tis Pity She's a Whore* and *The Broken Heart*. Boston, 1915.

────── *Ford's Debt to his Predecessors and Contemporaries; and his Contributions to the Decadence of the Drama*. Harvard Dissertation, 1906. MS. in Harvard University Library.

────── "A New Play by John Ford," *Modern Language Notes*, XXIII (1908), 245-9.

────── "Stella and The *Broken Heart*," *Publications of the Modern Language Association of America*, XXIV (1909), 274-85.

Shirley, James. *The Dramatic Works and Poems of James Shirley*. Ed. William Gifford and Alexander Dyce. London, 1833.

Sisson, C. J. *Lost Plays of Shakespeare's Age*. Cambridge, 1936.

Stoll, E. E. "Shakspere, Marston, and the Malcontent Type," *Modern Philology*, III (1906), 281-303.

Swinburne, A. C. "John Ford," *The Fortnightly Review,* XVI (1871), 42-63.

―――― *John Ford* (Sonnet). In *Tristram of Lyonesse and Other Poems,* p. 284. London, 1882.

―――― Prologue to *The Broken Heart.* In *A Channel Passage and Other Poems,* p. 192. London, 1904.

Sykes, H. Dugdale. "John Ford's Posthumous Play : 'The Queen,' " and "John Ford the Author of 'The Spanish Gipsy,' " *Sidelights on Elizabethan Drama.* Oxford, 1924.

Thomason, George. *Catalogue of the Pamphlets, Books, Newspapers, and Manuscripts Relating to the Civil War, the Commonwealth, and Restoration, Collected by George Thomason, 1640-1661.* London, 1908.

Tourneur, Cyril. *The Works of Cyril Tourneur.* Ed. Allardyce Nicoll. London [1930].

Turner, W. J. " 'Tis Pity She's a Whore," *The London Mercury,* VII (1923), 534-6.

Walley, H. R. *The Malcontent; a Study of the Elizabethan Dramatic Figure as an Expression and Emanation of the Temper of the Age.* Princeton Dissertation, 1924. MS. in Princeton University Library.

Ward, A. W. Article, "John Ford," *Encyclopaedia Britannica.*

―――― *A History of English Dramatic Literature to the Death of Queen Anne.* New York. 1899.

Webster, John. *The Complete Works of John Webster.* Ed. F. L. Lucas. London, 1927.

Williamson, J. Bruce. *The History of The Temple, London.* London, 1924.

Wolff, Max. *John Ford ein Nachahmer Shakespeare's.* Heidelberg, 1880.

X. X. "John Ford, the Dramatist," *Notes and Queries,* Ser. IV, Vol. XI (1873), 403.